Bright Ideas
for Managing the
Positive Classroom

PETER CLUTTERBUCK

Crown House Publishing Limited
www.crownhouse.co.uk

First published by Blake Education in 2001.

Original ISBN 1 86509 777 2

Current edition published 2005, reprinted 2005, 2007 and 2010 by
Crown House Publishing Ltd
Crown Buildings, Bancyfelin, Carmarthen, Wales, SA33 5ND, UK
www.crownhouse.co.uk

and

Crown House Publishing Company LLC
6 Trowbridge Drive, Suite 5, Bethel, CT 06801, USA
www.crownhousepublishing.com

British Library of Cataloguing-in-Publication Data
A catalogue entry for this book is available from the British Library.

10-digit ISBN 1904424511
13-digit ISBN 978-190442451-2

LCCN 2004111443

Printed and bound by
Gutenberg Press, Malta

Contents

Getting to Know Each Other Better

TO THE TEACHER

Early days

A new school year: for you, a new class; for the students, a new teacher. The students eagerly await your first words and actions.

Learning their individual names quickly is a great start as it sends a clear message to students that you are genuinely interested in them.

In the 'Early days' section you'll find some simple, short activities, adaptable to all primary or elementary levels, to help you all get to know each other better.

Through the year

Now you know each other's names and faces, there is much more to know about each individual student if a caring, supportive and growth promoting environment is to be created.

Students develop most effectively in an environment in which they feel safe and trust other class members and you – the teacher. Students want their ideas, thoughts and feelings to be valued; and a place where they can express them openly without fear of derision or ridicule. This occurs when they are provided with encouragement, affection and support.

The 'Through the year' activities will help you to get to know your class members better. They are simple, non-threatening and fun, and adaptable to all primary or elementary levels.

Early Days

Guess a name

Tell the students you are going to play a name guessing game. Explain that you will call out a name and if someone is called by that name, they must stand, say good morning to you and introduce themselves. Make sure that you have told the class your name and written it up so they can respond appropriately.

For example:

Teacher: *'Jack!'*

Jack, who is in the class, stands and introduces himself:

'Good morning (Mrs Harris). My name is Jack.'

If you make a correct guess of a name you score a point. If there is no student by that name, then the class scores a point.

15 MINUTES

Student introductions

In this activity a selected student stands and introduces him or herself and then introduces another student whom he or she knows in the class.

For example:

'Hello, my name is Michael and this is my friend David.'

David then introduces a student he knows. And so on around the class.

15 MINUTES

Rhyming names

Say a word at random and ask the students whose first names rhyme with the word to stand up and introduce themselves.

For example: *Ferry.*

'Good morning, I'm Gerry Naismith.'

'Good morning, my name is Terry Smith.'

10 MINUTES

Jumbled names

You will need to have studied the class register beforehand to do this activity.

Write given names on the blackboard in a jumbled form.

For example: *y a S l l.*

Point to each name in turn. When *Sally* recognises her name she stands and tells the class something about herself, such as: '*Hello, my name is Sally Cockroft. I am seven. My favourite television show is* Neighbours.'

15 MINUTES

Identification cards

Identification cards can easily be prepared using a little imagination. Photocopy enough so that each student has one to complete.

They should have spaces for *name, age, colour of eyes, colour of hair, things I like, things I dislike, my favourite food, my favourite activity, other special things about me.* Include space for a self-portrait or to attach a photograph.

Fold the card so it can sit neatly displayed on the student's desk.

See photocopiable resource on page 14.

20 MINUTES

Guess who it is

On a sheet of paper each student writes a brief description of him or herself, but does not include his or her name.

For example:

I have short brown hair. My eyes are blue. I like to collect stamps. My favourite sport is cricket.

Collect each one and shuffle them. Then distribute them to the students at random, who in turn read each one aloud. You or other students must guess who is the student being described.

10 MINUTES

Name game

Some students, if they are new to the school or if the class is made up of students from various classes from the previous year, may not be aware of the names of their classmates. Tell students you want to know all their names and that it is important for them to know the names of others.

Introduce the activity along these lines:

'We are going to have a short activity. I want you to walk around the room and introduce yourself to someone you don't know. Tell them your name and a little about yourself. For example – your favourite food, sport, hobby or television programme. You may find you have a lot in common!'

15 MINUTES

No errs

You will need a watch with a second hand, a stop watch or a student who can act as the 'seconds counter'.

Selected students must close their eyes and name as many other students in the class as they can, in 15 seconds, without saying 'Er' or 'Um'.

For example:

'I know Ben, Charlene, Rishi, Naomi, … Er…'

Now it is the next student's turn.

10 MINUTES

Starters

For younger students a name game can be combined with letter names.

Write a letter on the board, such as 'A'.

All the students say it together. Now students whose names begin with 'A' stand and introduce themselves.

For example:

'My name begins with 'A' – my name is Adam.'

'My name begins with 'A' – my name is Alice.'

Continue through the alphabet in this way.

For older students use opportunities that arise during this activity to acquaint them with other subject areas.

For example:

Q *Why do our names begin with capital letters?*

A *Because they are proper nouns.*

Q *Why are months and days written with capital letters?*

A *Because they are named after people or gods from ancient times.*

5 MINUTES

Riddles and rhymes

Ask your students to sit on the floor in a circle.

Start by saying: *'I am (Ms Smith).'*

The first student on your left says: *'I am Lucy and this is (Ms Smith).'*

The next student around the circle says: *'I am Bruno and this is Lucy and this is (Ms Smith).'*

The next student on the left then says: *'I am Robyn and this is Bruno and this is Lucy and this is (Ms Smith).'*

The process is continued around the circle until the last person has repeated everyone's name.

Last letters

Each student says his or her name, and adds a word that describes something about him or herself, or something he or she likes. The trick is that this word must start with the last letter of the student's name!

For example:

'My name is Mariko. I have olive skin.'

'My name is Paul and I am lucky.'

'My name is Sam and I like marmite.'

Through The Year

Questionnaires

Questionnaires provide an opportunity for students to express their thoughts and feelings. Make the questions open ended and don't make it compulsory for students to share their answers.

See photocopiable resources on pages 15–17.

10 MINUTES

Things I'm proud of

All students enjoy expressing pride in something they have done, or own. Provide opportunities for students to write or tell you about things they are proud of.

For example:

'*My favourite possession is ...*'

'*Something I have done for my parents is ...*'

'*Something I have done to earn pocket money is ...*'

Ask if they have any plans arising from the event, activity or object they describe.

10 MINUTES

My home

Ask your students to draw the floor plan of their homes. When they have completed their drawings, ask each one to take the other members of the group on a guided tour through their home, describing all the rooms, the furniture in them, and where their family eat, sleep, watch television and so on.

30 MINUTES

A letter to me

Ask the students to write letters to themselves in which they express their thoughts and feelings about school, friends, pets, the world in general and so on.

You could give them a worksheet simply headed 'Dear Me' and ask them to continue on from there.

15 MINUTES

My shield

Make enough photocopies of an outline of a shield for each student to have one.

Alternatively, ask them to fold a piece of A4 paper into quarters.

Now ask the students to draw four things about themselves, one in each section. They could include such things as:

1 Something I am good at.

2 My favourite possession.

3 The happiest moment I have had in the last year.

4 Something I'd like to be able to do better.

Suggest topics relevant to your students.

See photocopiable resource on page 18.

10 MINUTES

My own flag

You will need a copy of the national flag. Display the flag in the classroom and discuss with your students what its symbols represent.

Explain that every country has a flag and the different parts of it represent something that is important to the people of that country.

Now explain that today they are going to draw their own, personal flag and make symbols for things about themselves.

Encourage the students to use symbols that identify friendships, school, home, special moments, careers, goals in life and so on.

When the flags are completed, the students can (if they wish to) share the meanings of the symbols they have drawn with the rest of the class.

15 MINUTES

What it means to me

Divide some large sheets of paper into sections (or use the board). Make sure there is one section for each student.

Now ask your students to draw something that is meaningful to them on their section – it could be a prize possession, something liked or disliked or something they are concerned about.

In turn, ask the students to explain their drawing and why it has meaning for them.

20 MINUTES

What would I do?

Provide some real-life situations and encourage students to suggest logical and practical solutions.

For example:

1 You want to help a classmate who hasn't got any friends.

2 You want to help a new student who has recently arrived from another country and can't speak English very well.

3 You want to help a friend who is always getting into trouble and being sent to the headteacher.

4 You want to buy your mother a present for her birthday at the end of the month. You have saved £5 but the present costs £15.

Divide the class into small groups and ask each group to consider the same question and then report their responses to the whole class.

Alternatively, each group could look at a different problem.

30 MINUTES

This is mine

Ask students to bring to school some object that is meaningful to them, to share with the class. Give them a few days to think about the object they would like to bring in.

To help students understand what you mean, bring something to school yourself that you can share with them.

For example:

'These earrings I'm wearing were given to me by my parents for my eighteenth birthday. Whenever I wear them I'm reminded of my parents and the happy times we have together.'

If appropriate, allow the students to handle your special object and add other comments: *'When I wear them I get a good feeling.'*

Now encourage your students to bring something of their own to school. Tell them you'd like them to share something special of theirs with the class.

Ask the students to sit in a circle when they are sharing their objects. You may decide to choose one or two students a day, over a period of time, to share their objects.

15 MINUTES

Fold here

Draw something special to you here.

ID Card

I am

....

Age ....

Colour of eyes ....

Colour of hair ....

Things I like ....

Things I dislike ....

My favourite food ....

My favourite activity ....

Other special things about me ....

....

....

Questionnaire: Who am I?

Five words that describe me are:

1 ....   4 ....

2 ....   5 ....

3 ....

My friends are:

....

What I like best about school is:

....

....

What I don't like about school is:

....

....

If I could be anyone else I would be ....

because ....

In 10 years' time I'd like to be:

....

....

Questionnaire: My feelings

I like it when:

....

....

I don't like it when:

....

....

If I were grown up I would:

....

....

I get scared when:

....

....

I feel sad when:

....

....

If I could change something it would be:

....

....

Questionnaire: Who am I?

List five words that best describe you:

1 .... 4 ....

2 .... 5 ....

3 ....

What do you like about school?

....

....

What do you dislike about school?

....

....

What's your favourite things to do outside school?

....

....

....

Your favourite band?   Your favourite book?

....

What do you want to be doing 20 years from now?

....

....

My shield

The House of:

....

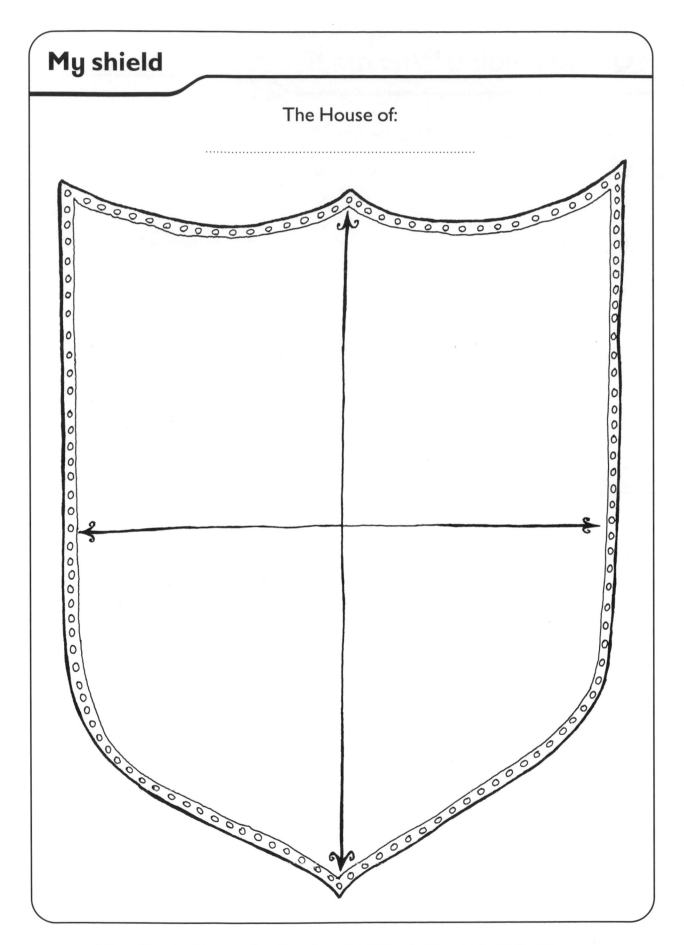

Activities for the First 10 Minutes of the Day

TO THE TEACHER

School trip money to be collected and recorded!

Lots of administration that must be completed!

Need a little time to get everything done?

Here are some activities that need no preparation and will keep the students occupied while you go about the administration and tasks of classroom teaching. Nevertheless, these activities are productive at any time of the day.

Passing messages

A selected student creates a sentence. He or she then whispers it to another student. From here it is whispered from individual to individual around the room.

The idea is to see if the message can remain intact.

Through this activity emphasise to the students the need to listen carefully and speak clearly.

'What would I do?' stories

You need to have some prepared scenarios and situations.

Give the class a scenario and ask one student: *'What would you do?'*

The student must explain his or her reaction to the situation.

For example:

How to cook a batch of sausages for 100 people.

What I'd do if I was chased by a dinosaur.

Alphabet animals

Ask the students to write the alphabet on the left-hand side of a sheet of paper. Then ask them to write the name of a living creature that begins with each letter.

For example: *A – ant*
                B – bear
                C – cow
                D – dog

Letter start

Ask the students to write a word that begins with each letter of the alphabet that spells the name of the day.

For example: *FRIDAY – fish, rock, ink, dog, ant, yellow.*

Alphabet foods

In this activity students are challenged to remember lists of words.

One student begins with something he or she ate that begins with '*a*'.

For example: '*I ate an apple.*'

The next player says: '*I ate an apple …*' then adds a food beginning with '*b*'.

For example: '*I ate an apple and a bun.*'

The next player repeats the whole sentence adding something beginning with '*c*'.

For example: '*I ate an apple and a bun and a cake.*' And so on.

The activity continues until players cannot remember all the things that have been eaten.

This can also be played using other categories.

Doodling away

Each student will need a sheet of A4 paper.

Ask the students to make a simple doodle or picture on the paper, then pass it on for the next student to add to it.

Each doodle or drawing keeps getting passed around the room until all students have added something to each other's doodles.

Shopping A to Z

This activity begins with one student stating: '*I went shopping and I bought an apple.*'

The next student repeats the sentence, but the item purchased must begin with '*b*' and so on through the alphabet.

Longest lists

The object of this activity is for groups of students to come up with the longest list of items on a given subject.

Some subjects might include:

- *Types of birds*
- *Animals*
- *Fruit*
- *Vegetables*
- *Given names*
- *Countries.*

You could also choose a subject that is being studied by the class.

Sentence building

The activity begins with one student who starts the sentence by saying a suitable opening word such as '*A*', '*The*', '*I*' and so on. This student then points to another student who must repeat that word and add another of his or her own, '*A dog*'.

He or she points to another student who repeats these two words and also adds another, '*A dog barked*'.

This continues around the class until students can no longer add meaningful words and then someone starts another sentence.

Remembering actions

A selected student performs a number of single actions, such as coughing, jumping, then clapping hands.

Other students in turn try to repeat all the actions in their correct order.

Rhyme times

For this activity the students work in pairs or groups.

Each pair or group is given a word. They must then compile a list of words that rhyme with this word.

For example:

Spoon – moon, soon, balloon.

Who tapped me?

Select two or three students to stand at the front of the class.

The rest of the class sit at tables with their heads down, eyes closed and thumbs in the air. The selected students move quietly around the room and each one taps one student on their raised thumb.

When they return to the front, the students who were tapped must guess who touched them.

If their guess is correct, they swap places.

This game can also be played using three random objects to be placed on students' desks!

Doggie Doggie

The students sit in a circle and one student, who is 'Doggie', sits in the centre with his or her eyes closed.

The students in the circle pass an object such as a pen or book behind their backs. At a given signal 'Doggie' opens his or her eyes

and the students in the circle chant, *'Doggie, Doggie, who's got the bone?'*

The student who is 'Doggie' must guess who is hiding the object. Once 'Doggie' has identified the correct person, they swop places and the activity starts again.

Who's missing?

A selected student leaves the room while another student hides in the classroom.

On his or her return, the student who was outside guesses who is hiding.

Adding letters

You will need a list of ten four-letter words. On the board, write only the first and last letters of each, or the middle two letters.

Ask the students to complete the words by adding any letters that fit and make sense.

Mix and match

You will need some old newspapers.

Cut the pages of a newspaper into halves, thirds or quarters. Jumble them up and distribute them to the students.

The students must find the other parts of the paper to complete a full sheet.

Dictionary puzzle

Select a student to find an interesting word in the dictionary. He or she tells the rest of the class what the word begins with and also its dictionary definition.

For example: *'This word begins with "w" and means a type of tree that often grows near water.'*

The other students either write down the answer or call it out. The student with the first correct answer swaps places.

Jumbled words

You will need to prepare a list of 20 four- or five-letter words.

Write these on the board, jumbling up the letters. Challenge the students to rearrange the letters to make the correct words.

The words can be chosen according to a theme, for example names of vegetables or animals.

Anagrams

You will need a prepared list of words to write on the board.

Ask the students to rearrange all the letters of each word to make another word or words.

For example:

Meat – tame, team, mate

Shore – horse

Acrosses

Ask students to choose a five-letter word and write its letters vertically down one side of the page, then backwards down the other side.

The aim of the activity is to find a word to bridge the gap between each pair of letters.

For example:

e	n	d	o	w
l	a	s	s	o
b	u	l		b
o	w			l
w	h	e	r	e

Wood, fabric, plastic

The students work in pairs or small groups.

Ask them to draw three columns on a piece of paper and label them:

'Wood', 'Fabric' and 'Plastic'.

Now ask the students to list as many objects in the classroom as they can that belong to each category.

For example: *Wood – pencil, chair, table, windowsill.*

Place names

You will need some maps, local street directories and/or atlases.

Allow the students time to explore the maps for strange or novel place names. Have them make up stories describing how they think the place got its name.

For example:

- *Newcastle*
- *Wolf Point*
- *Rockford.*

Ask students to invent names of their own, including an explanation for the name.

Tag

The students stand and spread themselves around the room. Ask a number of questions. The first student to respond correctly is able to take one step in any direction. If this means he or she can touch another player, the person who has been tagged is 'out'. The game continues until only one person is left.

This is a popular game, making a bright start to the day!

Growing words

Ask each student to write his or her name on the top of a sheet of paper. The letters should be well spread out.

Under each letter they must write a two-letter word beginning with that letter if they can.

Below that, they then write a three-letter word beginning with that letter, then a four-letter word and so on.

For example:

G	R	A	E	M	E
go		at		me	
get	rat	ape	end	mat	ear
goat	rung	able	eggs	mast	even
groan	round	apple	egret	moist	every

Sentence days

Challenge the students to make up a sentence where each word begins with the letters that spell the day.

For example: *MONDAY – Meg only notices dogs aboard yachts.*

Dictionary search

You will need a prepared list of words to search for in the dictionary.

Ask the students to search through their dictionaries to find, for example:

- *The longest word that begins with 'e' (or any other letter).*
- *Five animals that begin with 'b'.*
- *The last two words that begin with 'p'.*

Making words

On the board, write a long word.

For example: *Christmas, Constantinople,* or *arithmetic.*

Working in pairs or small groups, the students make as many words as possible from the given word.

For example: *Arithmetic – metric, chair, them* and so on.

When I'm famous

As a short activity, ask the students to practise developing the signature they will use when they become famous!

No vowels

Challenge the students to write a sentence or a story without using a specific vowel.

For example:

- *No 'e's – A man saw a dog in a paddock.*

- *No 'a's – The two fine old beds were sold over the weekend.*

- *No 'i's – See how many of these you can make!*

- *No 'o's – What will happen when it rains?*

- *No 'u's – It will be wet all weekend, so they say!*

Things I would need

Ask the students to compile lists of things they would need if they were undertaking a particular activity. This could be completed in pairs or small groups.

For example:

- *Things I would need to go to the moon.*

- *Things I would need to take on a fishing trip.*

Twenty questions

A student chooses a certain object but does not say what it is.

The rest of the class then question the student to determine what it is. They are allowed to ask only twenty questions.

The person being questioned replies using only *'Yes'*, *'No'* or *'Sometimes'*.

With practice, students become quite skilful in their choice of questions to narrow down the possibilities.

Word boxes

Working individually, in pairs or small groups, the students make as many words as possible using the letters written in a grid.

Older students must include in each word the letter in the middle box.

The word need not necessarily begin with that letter.

For example:

E	T	M
R	**S**	A
I	B	P

- *Stamp, mast, stir, rest* and so on.

These take only a moment to write on the board.

Last letter

One student says a word.

For example: *'Monkey'*.

He or she then points to another student who must say a word that begins with the last letter of the word.

For example: *'**Y**acht'*.

This student points to the next student, who gives a word starting with *'**t**'*, and so on around the class.

Word change

Write a single word, such as *FUN*, on the board.

Students come to the board in turn, rub out a letter and add a letter of their own to make a new word:

For example: *FUN → SUN → RUN → BUN → BUT → BAT → BAG → BIG → FIG → FOG → LOG* and so on.

Hangman

This is an old but popular game with all levels of students.

A student selects a word and, keeping it secret, writes on the board a dash for each letter.

The rest of the class call out letters and for each correct response the letter is written over the corresponding dash.

For an incorrect response the student draws a section of a scaffold.

Older students may wish to guess a proverb or short sentence.

Shapes

On the board, draw a large random shape.

Ask the students to look at it. Now, select a student to change it into something new by adding lines and details.

Add a line

Divide the class into two teams.

The first student of each team comes out to the board and draws a line.

The next student adds another, and so on, until a picture is formed.

See which team can produce the most original or funniest picture.

Directions

You, or a student, stand at the board with a piece of chalk.

A selected student describes how to draw a pre-determined object without revealing what that object is. He or she must give explicit instructions, explaining exactly where to start and stop drawing, the direction across the board and so on.

What is it?

You will need to divide the class into small groups.

One person from each group is given a drawing, which he or she takes back to the group and describes to the other members, without letting them see it. The person describing the picture must not tell the subject of the picture, and may only describe the shapes and lines it is made up of.

Each member of the group must try to draw what has been described.

Word make

Students draw a 4 × 4 grid on a sheet of paper.

You, or a selected student, call out letters at random. As each letter is called students write it down in the grid.

When the sixteen letters have been called the students count the number of words they have made. Words can run across the grid horizontally, vertically and diagonally.

Itemising

Name: ....

Task 1: The teacher will call out ten items. When the teacher has finished, pick up your pen and see if you can write down all ten items.

Task 2: The teacher will hold up ten objects and then hide them. See if you can remember and draw all ten objects.

1 ....   6 ....

2 ....   7 ....

3 ....   8 ....

4 ....   9 ....

5 ....   10 ....

1	2	3	4	5
6	7	8	9	10

The Attentive Classroom

TO THE TEACHER

The attentive classroom is one in which all the students feel they are an integral part of a cohesive group. The class teacher provides stimulating lessons and adds mystery and suspense to the teaching, while at the same time promoting active involvement. Teachers who continually work towards developing a strong, positive group feeling among the students will find them more attentive and more willing to participate in class activities.

LEARNING TO LISTEN

To promote an attentive classroom, the students must first be taught to 'listen', that is, they must be able to hear the information, then process it.

In the following pages you'll find games and activities that promote an attentive classroom and that are easily adaptable to all levels. They are focused on:

● developing listening skills in your students.

● actively using periods of silence in the classroom.

● encouraging creative noise.

The attentive 'word'

Use a key listening word as an attention grabber.

Select a word at the beginning of the week and use it to get the immediate attention of all students. Choose words that are unlikely to be said in normal conversation. When you say this word, all students must respond by stopping what they are doing and listening.

Award points to those students who are the quickest to respond.

The class can be loosely grouped into teams. The team that is first to respond to the attentive word is given points and the winning team is announced at the end of the week.

Reward the winning team members with such things as five minutes extra on the computer and so on.

Pair up

Ask the students to walk around the room to the rhythm of music.

When the music stops they must pair up with the nearest person. One of the pair asks the other three or more questions.

For example:

● *'What is your favourite food?'*

● *'What football team do you follow?'*

● *'What makes you sad?'*

When all the students have asked their questions and been given the answers, ask them to sit in a circle. Students describe their partner to show how well they listened.

Story time

1 Read a short story to students and then ask them to recall facts about it.

2 Make up a story in which you have deliberately inserted some little nonsense details. Ask the students to listen and find the nonsense parts.

For example:

'Yesterday when I walked to the supermarket I saw a flock of penguins flying overhead. When I paid for my shopping I gave the cashier three pound coins.'

3 Read out lists of words or numbers to the students. On a given signal, ask them to recall and write the lists on a sheet of paper, in the correct order.

For example:

Dog, cat, mule, zebra, horse.

Variety

Use a variety of ways to communicate with students to encourage them to listen and be attentive to the message you are giving.

1 **Whisper instructions**. The students will have to be very attentive to hear what you want them to do.

2 **Spell out the directions** you are giving:

T–A–K–E … O–U–T … Y–O–U–R … S–P–E–L–L–I–N–G … B–O–O–K–S

3 Communicate directions to students **using only your hands** (or other body language). For example: if you want the students to write down some spelling, point to the word 'spelling' on the blackboard and mime writing words in a book.

4 Instead of saying instructions, **write them on the board**. Alternatively, ask a question, such as 'What is a penguin?', by writing it down. Ask students who know the answer to write it on a sheet of paper and hold it up for you to see.

5 **Try mouthing directions**. Challenge students to 'read your lips' to discover what you are saying.

SILENCE

It is important to plan for deliberate periods of silence. Try to plan a relaxed silent activity to follow a boisterous one. Alternating periods of deliberate silence with more active noisy activities should be an integral part of every class programme.

Don't be afraid to allow students the odd moment to daydream. The student who is momentarily gazing out of the window or at the wall is journeying through the 'hidden curriculum'. All students need these delicious moments to become lost in the privacy of their own imaginations.

USSR

Many teachers use the first ten minutes after the lunch break for USSR (Uninterrupted Sustained Silent Reading).

During this time the entire class, including the teacher, reads material of their own choice in silence. Apart from the obvious benefit of reading, this activity also assists students to relax after the rigours of the lunch break and thus become more receptive to the afternoon's programme.

Time to reflect

If you are reading a story, fairytale, legend and so on, plan short breaks of deliberate silence at the end of each section. This allows the students time to reflect on the story or use their imaginations to conjure up some particular scene or happening.

In normal teaching, always plan short breaks of deliberate silence to allow the students to reflect on the subject matter or on some particular difficulty or aspect. At the end of the silence, ask students to comment on what they have learnt.

CREATIVE NOISE

Although unwanted noise must be kept to a minimum, creative noise is productive in the learning process. For example, many small group activities require active exchanges of communication and expression during which much important learning is occurring.

If students have been physically inactive for a period, follow this with an appropriate activity designed for them to make noise and let off steam. The following are some such activities.

Nicknames

Conduct a class discussion with the students about nicknames.

For example:

- *'What is a nickname that would make you feel good about yourself?'*

- *'What is a nickname that would make you feel bad?'*

- *'What would a classroom be like if everyone was given a nickname they liked or disliked?'*

Now ask students to give each other a nickname based on their strengths and positive qualities.

For example:

- A girl who is good at running might be called 'Radcliffe' or 'Holmes'.

- A boy who is good at football might be called 'Beckham' or 'Owen', and so on.

Problems and decisions

Problem solving and decision making is a fun activity that helps build a feeling of togetherness. These activities are for small groups of four to five students.

1 Pose a problem to each group and ask them to reach an agreed solution.

2 Provide a group of students with a list of occupations – nurse, doctor, teacher, lorry driver, policeman, firefighter and so on.

Ask each group to rate the occupations from most important to least important. One person records the results on a sheet of paper and reports their group's opinions back to the class.

Hello!

Ask the students to move around the room in a boisterous manner, such as marching, hopping and so on.

On a signal, the students must immediately stop and form a pair with the person nearest to them. They shake hands with that person saying, 'Hello!'. Each person then tells the other something they like to do and something they do not like to do.

On a given signal, the students move around the room again and go through the same procedure to find another partner.

At the end, question students and challenge them to remember what other members of the class like and dislike.

Favourite words

Spread a large piece of paper across the classroom floor. Using a felt pen, roughly divide it into equal (or near equal) spaces – one for each student.

In each space ask students to write their favourite word. When everyone has finished, ask them to explain why that word is their favourite.

Bragging

Bragging lets off steam and helps develop self-esteem.

Ask the students to form groups of four or five. Tell them that they each have one minute in which to brag about anything they feel like – achievements, awards, skills, a clever pet, their football team, things they have done well in or feel they are good at and so on.

At the end, ask the students to share their feelings about bragging. Ask:

- Did you enjoy boasting about yourself?
- Did you enjoy listening to others boasting?

Positive and negative

On the board, write a jumbled list of words expressing positive actions and negative actions, such as stealing, helping, bullying, supporting, whispering, clapping, pointing, smiling, hitting and so on.

Point to each word in turn.

- If it expresses a *negative* action, the students remain *silent*.
- If it expresses a *positive* action, they call out '*Positive*' at the top of their voices.

GAINING ATTENTION

The key to successful classroom management is for students to be active and interested participants in all education activities.

To achieve this you must first gain, then hold, their attention. Throughout this book you will find lots of games and activities that will assist.

Here are some ideas suitable for all primary levels.

And don't forget there are also lots of ideas for starter activities in the 'Activities for the First 10 Minutes of the Day' section.

Begin on a bright note!

Begin the day on a bright note with an interesting activity. This may be a dictionary activity, a quiz or a game of hangman. A well introduced activity will set a warm, stimulating learning pattern for the day.

For lots of starter activity ideas, see 'Activities for the First 10 Minutes of the Day'.

Directions directive

To ensure students are interested in what you are saying, present it in an interesting way.

For example: you may spell out directions: *'T–a–k–e … o–u–t … y–o–u–r … m–a–t–h–s … b–o–o–k–s'*

Smile

Don't forget to smile, and be prepared to laugh at yourself if you make an error. If students sense that you are happy and enjoy what you are doing – teaching them – then they are sure to enjoy your company!

Reinforce with sincerity

Reward and reinforce good behaviour with sincere words of appreciation, on the spot. The person you are addressing will feel appreciated and self-esteem will grow.

Always praise where praise is due!

Eye contact

When talking to students, either as a small group or to the whole class, make sure that they are looking at you and you at them.

To make sure all students are within your field of vision, stretch out your arms at about a 45° angle and ask them to sit within this area.

Names

Ensure you learn students' first names early on. Students tune in quickly when you are able to address them by name.

If you have difficulty remembering names, there are some tricks you can learn, as well as using name tags and asking students to sit according to a plan!

1 Try associating a characteristic of the student with his or her name.

For example: *talkative Ryan, red-haired Lisa, tall Mei Ling* and so on.

2 Alternatively, if you have a more visual memory, try making a rough sketch of the student and attributing his or her name to it.

Early finishers

Keep the students active and busy. Remember 'idle hands make mischief'. So have plenty of activities prepared and ready for the early finishers.

Interesting books

Build up a collection of interesting books. They may be picture books, books of interesting or humorous poems, short stories, jokes or anecdotes.

Take breaks to read items from them to your students.

'Some books are to be tasted, others to be swallowed and some few to be chewed and digested...'

Francis Bacon

Change the activity

If students are becoming restless, change the activity. You may be boring them or the activity may simply have gone on for too long.

You'll find lots of ideas for various activities in this book.

Don't shout!

Don't call out or shout directions over students' working noise. Noisy teachers make noisy students. If you need to explain something again, attract all the students' attention before saying what you want to say.

One way of doing this is to establish an 'attention grabber' or 'stop signal' in an enjoyable way. Do this early in the day.

Some examples are:

1 When you ring a bell, clap your hands or say a 'special word', students must sit up with their hands on their heads.

2 Alternatively, you might clap a given rhythm. When students hear this, they must stop, sit and clap the rhythm back.

Praise those who are first to be sitting and listening.

You now have their attention!

Getting back attention

If you see that a student's attention is wandering, consider:

- rephrasing what you have said in simpler terms.

- changing the pace of what you are saying.

- mentioning the name of the restless student, mid-sentence.

Keeping busy

Build up a stock of quick and easily adaptable activities to have at hand.

You will find lots of ideas throughout this book.

If the lesson is waning, have a short break for students to 'recharge their batteries'.

Goodies

1 Bring a bag of 'goodies' to school. It could contain interesting or strange objects.

   In breaks, students can choose one, describe it, handle it and put it away.

2 Alternatively, have a grab bag full of stickers that you can use to reward good workers or consistent helpers.

   Always reward positive behaviour!

Riddles and rhymes

Use poems, word plays, riddles, rhymes or jokes to gain students' attention.

When students are in the process of packing up, an interesting song or game will help speed up the slower ones among them.

Board

Use the board effectively. Bright coloured markers, novel lettering and meaningful diagrams or decorations all assist in grabbing the attention of students.

For lots of ideas, turn to 'Twenty Tips for Making the Board More Effective'.

Novel introductions

Think of novel ways to introduce topics that otherwise could be mundane.

For example: *'Conjunctions as joining words' – break a ruler in two then glue it together to show students how conjunctions join sentences.*

Show your interest

In spare moments, ask the students to tell you about their interests. Students who feel you are interested in them will undoubtedly become interested in what you have to say.

Remember to be a good listener.

Seating

Make sure all students are seated comfortably. A person who feels uncomfortable is unlikely to be involved or interested in what is being said.

Think about what comfort implies – is it that the chair and desk are the correct size, that the students are sitting in friendship groups or with their peers, that they are not squashed on top of each other on the floor?

A simple arrangement of furniture and people can make a huge difference to student attentiveness.

Be spontaneous

If, during a lesson, a general point of interest in another topic arises and you feel the students have a genuine interest to explore it, then allow them to do so.

For example: you may be taking a lesson on 'Food Chains' when one student mentions an adventure he or she had with a snake when camping. This may lead to a discussion of snakes and the treatment of snake bites.

Remember to bring the discussion back to the lesson topic when the general point of interest has been explored.

Speaking up

Modulate the tone of your voice. Use a voice that is appropriate to the task at hand. When reading a story or report, explaining or asking questions, add interest with the expression you use. People of all ages will lose interest in, for example, a constant high-pitched voice or a continually monotonous tone.

Remember: It has been said that children can concentrate on a particular topic for only one to one-and-a-half minutes for every year of their age.

Don't talk for too long!

Innovative Ways to Use the Classroom

TO THE TEACHER

Apart from their own homes, school students spend the majority of their waking hours inside a classroom. The classroom must provide a warm, welcoming, exciting, stimulating environment in which students feel both happy and secure.

At the end of the day you may gasp and feel your classroom looks like a disaster area rather than a place of ordered learning. Don't be depressed: a cooperative group of students will only take five minutes to have it looking tidy again!

What you may label a mess is usually the result of active, productive and successful learning activities. The classroom with the 'lived-in look' will provide far better opportunities for the development of students physically, emotionally and academically than those cold, sterile ones in which spontaneity and active participation in learning activities are frowned upon. Remember: just as a house may not be a home, a classroom may not be a centre of learning.

The following are some ideas for enhancing the space in which you teach.

Share table

This is extremely important for lower primary classes. Have a special table or bench set aside where students can display objects that have special meaning to them.

The objects may be as different as the cocoon of a moth and a doll brought from overseas. Encourage students to tell the others about their special possession.

Students' work displays

Keep a continual display of students' work which is regularly removed and replaced.

For lower and middle primary students, have a 'star improvers' spot where handwriting samples and so on show a definite improvement.

For example:

> ### *Congratulations to*
> (student's name)...
>
> From this (old sample of work)
>
> to this (new sample of work)
>
> ***WOW!***

Book displays

Invite a local bookseller to display new books in your room. Invite parents along to buy a book to donate to your class or library. Glue a certificate in each book stating the name of the family who donated it.

Other displays

Apart from students' work, also consider displaying things such as new books to read, notices of coming events and so on. Remember to keep the displays used by students at eye level.

A fishing net suspended from the ceiling provides a great vehicle for hanging all kinds of work and other objects using paper clips or pegs.

Displays of other classes' work

Invite another class (or classes) to display their work in your room. Invite students from these classes to come and view the display and discuss it with your students.

Alternatively, if your class has a special display, invite other classes to view it.

Discovery box

Have a large wooden box in the classroom in which there are old toys, torches, car parts and so on. Allow students to pull them apart and put them back together in spare moments.

Place mats

To brighten up the classroom have students decorate their own desk tops by making colourful patterns or scenes on sheets of light cardboard, cut to size and firmly stuck onto the desk top.

Swap day

Invite the rest of the school to your classroom for a swap day. Students can bring their swap cards, stamp collections, old toys and so on to swap with other students during the lunch break.

Creative board

You can make the board a real centre of attention and activity in a variety of ways.

Consider:

- using different writing styles.

- having a dedicated 'Kids' Section' for ideas and comments written by students.

- writing a 'Thought for the Week' in a special place each Monday morning.

- working on a 'Mystery Drawing' that has a bit added to it each day so that by the end of the week the students can work out the mystery.

You'll find lots of other ideas in 'Twenty Tips for Making the Board More Effective'.

A poetree

Obtain a medium-sized branch from a tree. Place it in a paint tin filled with soil or sand so it is stable. Ask the students to paint and decorate it. Use the tree to display students' poems, stories and so on.

This activity is a must for lower primary classes.

Dressing up box

Young students enjoy dressing up. A source of old clothes is also useful when the class is dramatising stories and plays.

Parents are usually happy to donate clothing they no longer want. Old wigs, strings of beads, artificial pearls, bangles and bracelets are all useful.

A must for younger students.

Feeding table

If your classroom has ample window space, consider erecting a small, simple feeding table for birds just outside the room. Often just a board attached to the window ledge will suffice. Suitable food can be placed on the ledge each day so the students can enjoy watching the birds.

Puppet theatre

A puppet theatre can be easily constructed from a large cardboard box with one side cut out. Puppets can be made from paper bags, socks, paper plates, cardboard or cut-out figures mounted on rulers or sticks.

Learning centres

Develop learning centres around the classroom. These consist of working spaces for students and storage spaces for materials and activities. Natural dividers can be erected using tables, wall units, portable book shelves and so on.

Each centre should provide students with the opportunity to practise their skills. Make sure the various resources are easily accessible and easy to return to their storage areas so that other class members are not disturbed.

Some examples of learning centres are:

- **Writing Centre** – provide different kinds of paper, pens and other writing tools, samples of different kinds of writing, a comfortable desk and chair.

- **Reading Centre** – provide a wide selection of reading materials, a comfortable chair, good lighting, and as far as possible make sure students are not disturbed.

- **Explore Centre** – provide a wide range of things to explore and ideas for where to go if you are looking for more information. Be lateral in your thinking when equipping this centre.

- **Quiet Centre** – provide a private space, comfortable seating, a variety of peaceful decorations. This centre provides an opportunity for students to have some 'time out'.

Ask the students to bring their own books, magazines, pictures and so on to contribute to the learning centres.

Safe haven

Students should be aware that the classroom belongs to all of them. Less physically robust students or those with genuine emotional stress may wish to use it as a 'safe haven' from time to time – a place to which they can withdraw when they feel under stress in the playground.

Be aware of school policy statements regarding student access to the classroom – your presence may be required during these times or you may be able to make some form of compromise with the headteacher or other staff members.

Special days

Football finals, Remembrance Day and so on provide opportunities for students to decorate the room.

For example:

- Have a Footy Final Day in which students decorate the room in the colours of their football teams. Display photos of their favourite players around the room.

- For Remembrance Day display medals or build a small cenotaph to use during remembrance ceremonies.

Overseas day

Use your room to celebrate or learn about the customs and traditions of another country.

For example: Prepare for American Independence Day. Decorate the room with red, white and blue stripes and stars. As an art activity, students could make a model of the Statue of Liberty using clay or another malleable material.

White elephant sale

Use your room for a white elephant sale to raise money for social service projects. Ask the students to bring along items that they no longer want, to sell to other students. Donate the proceeds to a suitable project, chosen by a class vote.

Theme times

If you are covering a theme in your class then decorate the room to add atmosphere. Use art and craft time to create the decorations.

For example:

- A bit of imagination can transform your room into a 'Fairyland' or a 'Giant's Castle' to help create atmosphere for a theme of 'Nursery Rhyme' or 'Fairy Tale'.

- For 'American Pioneers', the whole room could be transformed into the inside of a pioneer cottage. Use painted cardboard to simulate logs and so on.

- For 'Space', transform part of the room to resemble the inside of a space shuttle and decorate other parts with mobiles of the galaxy and planets with rings and moons.

Team teaching

Team teaching can be a rewarding experience for you and your students. It is a good way to share teaching talents or areas of interest with a larger group of students.

The demands of team teaching are greater in some respects, as you will have to get to know more students. However, if it is well thought out and there are complementary skills between you and your teaching partner/s, it can also allow for an effective use of resources. For effective team teaching, you will need to cooperate willingly and share classroom tasks and materials with other members of the team.

There are numerous forms of organisation in any team teaching situation:

- You may spend the morning with your students in your classroom working on specific skills areas. During the afternoon students can work in any of the rooms.

- You may divide curriculum areas among the teaching partners to tap into particular strengths. If you are teaching English and Geography, keep specialist teaching materials for those curriculum areas in your classroom. Other teachers in the team should keep specialist materials for their subject/s in their home classrooms.

Effective team teaching must be agreed to and supported by the school management team. For more ideas see 'Activities that Involve 2, 3 and 4 Year Groups'.

USING PLANTS

Some teachers may be dismissive of such an activity as growing plants in the classroom, but the enthusiasm generated and the results can be surprising. Remember your young days of growing seeds in a saucer with moist cotton wool or kitchen towel? Today's students are just as fascinated by such a simple activity.

Growing plants not only serves to brighten the classroom, but also provides students with a variety of valuable learning experiences, broadening their awareness of the environment and offering a unique way to introduce experiences that encompass other curriculum areas.

Maths

For young students, counting out seeds to be placed in a dish provides valuable number experience.

Older students can be introduced to the concept of percentages and fractions by recording germination results.

For example:

I planted 100 wheat seeds.

65 of these seeds germinated.

My percentage of germination is $\dfrac{65}{100} = 65\%$.

Handwriting and written expression

For handwriting and written expression, students can record the daily or weekly growth patterns of the seeds. The information gathered can form the basis of a written report.

Science

As a science unit, students may wish to experiment with the plants to observe what happens if:

- *The seeds are placed in a dark place such as a classroom cupboard.*

- *The seeds are planted in different soils (collected by students).*

- *The seeds are placed in direct sunlight or a cold spot such as the school refrigerator.*

- *Plant nutrients are added to some dishes.*

- *The seeds are placed in water alone. This may lead to a study of hydroponics by the more interested students.*

Alternatively, students may wish to grow some exotic plants such as insect-eating plants. These are easily purchased and clear instructions for their care are provided on the labels.

PSHE

For PSHE, students will enjoy growing and eating mung bean or alfalfa (lucerne) sprouts, which are rich in vitamins and minerals.

If students maintain their interest in growing plants, let them develop their own small plot in the school garden. This may take the form of an attractive display of flowering annuals or even a small market garden. The vegetables grown may be sold to raise money for some school project.

The following are some suggestions for how to create your own classroom greenroom. These activities are suitable to all primary levels. All the materials you will need are listed at the beginning of each activity.

Carrot fern

You will need:

- large carrots – ask your students to bring one each from home

- a sharp knife

- some thin wire cut into 20 cm lengths

- access to water.

Carefully cut off the bottom two-thirds of the carrot and discard. (Perhaps your students might like to eat the leftover carrot!)

Turn the top piece (sprouting end) upside down and scoop out the inside with the knife.

Now push the wire through the carrot and hang it in a position where it will get some sunlight. The scooped-out portion of the carrot must be kept filled with water.

In time, the carrot will be covered with pretty fern-like foliage that should last a month or so.

Indoor orchard

You will need:

- some apple, pear, grapefruit or orange seeds – ask your students to collect some from home

- a jar

- a small quantity of potting compost or other suitable soil

- a potting dish of some kind

- access to water.

Soak the seeds in a jar of water for two or three days, until they sink to the bottom.

When this happens, plant the seeds in the dish of potting compost or soil and place in a sunny position.

If the seeds are watered regularly, in about ten days you should have a small orchard of thriving fruit trees.

As the seedlings grow in size they should be placed in larger containers and eventually planted out.

Combination garden

You will need:

- various whole vegetables – ask your students to bring some from home
- a shallow dish
- some small pebbles
- a sharp knife
- access to water.

Interesting displays can be developed by combining different vegetables in the same container.

Fill a shallow dish with the small pebbles and water. Trim the vegetables, leaving about 3 cm of flesh on each. Place these in the dish and water them regularly.

The contrast between the colours and shapes of the different leaves makes a lovely show.

Potato and onion plants

You will need:

- small- to medium-sized potatoes and/or onions – ask your students to bring one each from home
- a jar for each potato/onion
- a packet of toothpicks
- access to water.

1 Ask the students to stick toothpicks around the edge of the potato. This will allow it to rest on the rim of the jar. Fill the jar with water until it covers the bottom third of the

potato. The jar should be positioned so it gets daylight but not direct sun.

2 Onions can be grown in a similar way. Students can peel the dry, outer skin away from the onions and push toothpicks into the flesh. Fill the jar with water and place the onion root end down in the water, so that the bottom third is covered.

If the jar is positioned in sunlight, the onion will grow light green leaves. If the jar is placed in a dark spot, the leaves will be yellow.

Peas and beans

You will need:

- pea or bean seeds
- shallow dishes and a small quantity of potting compost or soil

  or

- blotting paper, cotton wool and a clear glass jar
- access to water.

Peas and beans are easily grown in shallow dishes filled with suitable soil or potting compost.

A more interesting way to grow them is to place some blotting paper so it covers the inside walls of a clear, glass jar. Now fill the centre of the jar with cotton wool. When this is done, place the seeds between the blotting paper and the wall of the jar and pour water over the cotton wool in the centre. After a few days the seeds will sprout and the students will be able to observe the growth of the roots and shoots through the clear glass.

Pineapple plant

You will need:

- a fresh pineapple
- some small pebbles
- a small quantity of potting compost or other suitable soil
- a sharp knife
- access to water.

Cut the top off the pineapple, leaving about 3 cm of flesh. Now place the pebbles in the dish and cover with about 3 cm of potting compost or soil. Press the crown of the pineapple into the soil, and water regularly.

If the container is placed in direct sunlight for several hours a day, roots will soon develop and new leaves will begin to appear.

Grafting and budding

Do you have a keen gardener, horticulturalist or florist in your parent group? If not, there's bound to be someone with practical gardening skills in the local community.

Invite an experienced gardener or florist to the school to teach students the art of grafting or budding smaller plants and trees. Students may wish to try growing three or more different types of plum or apple on one tree.

Melon seeds

You will need:

- melon seeds

- a shallow dish

- a small quantity of potting compost or other suitable soil

- sticks

- small lengths of wool or twine

- access to water.

Melons are all quite easily grown and make a fine show. Plant the seeds in a dish of soil and water them regularly. In about two weeks, sprouts will push through the soil.

As the plants become taller, place sticks next to each one and tie with a piece of wool.

Salt garden

You will need:

- a large, shallow dish

- packet of salt

- teaspoons

- tablespoonful of vinegar

- stones

- access to water.

A salt garden can create a lot of interest in students of all ages. It is also simple and easy to make.

Fill the dish with water and allow the students to add salt, a teaspoonful at a time. Stir until it dissolves completely. Let them continue to add salt until no more will dissolve. When this is completed, add a tablespoonful of vinegar. The students can now fill the dish with stones or pieces of coal and leave it to stand overnight.

The next day, masses of salt crystals will have covered the stones, creating an interesting effect.

Twenty Tips for Making the Board More Effective

Presentation Ideas

Creative writing

When writing words, write them in novel, interesting ways. The way you write the word can often reflect its meaning. For example:

We saw a **fat** pig.

$$\frac{frac}{tions}$$

This can help students to remember the spelling of words.

Fantastic frames

Add colourful frames around headings.

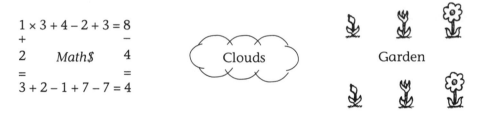

Thought for the week

Supply a regular 'Thought for the Week' each Monday for the students to contemplate during the week.

Example: *I cried because I had no shoes until I met a man who had no feet.*

You will find more thoughts on page 67.

Graffiti segment

Have a graffiti segment reserved for the students to write and draw in during free time.

Call it something they can relate to such as Kids' Space or Graffiti Garage.

Mystery drawing

At the beginning of each week start a drawing on some part of the board. Each day add a few more lines and let the students guess what it might be.

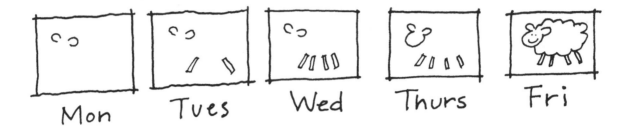

Make a sentence

Begin a sentence on Monday. Each day ask the students to add a word or two of their own, until the sentence is finished on Friday. This is also a useful language activity.

Mon	Tue	Wed	Thurs	Fri
The dog	ran	fast	to chase	the stick.

For a variation of 'Make a sentence', start a sentence and ask for suggestions for other words that mean the same thing, so you have more than one sentence being built.

Mon	Tue	Wed	Thurs	Fri
The dog	ran	fast	to chase	the stick.
The canine	raced	like a flash	to run after	the twig.

Presentation Ideas/Games

Positive Space

Keep a space on the board open for the students to record their experiences of positive behaviour on behalf of other members of the class.

For example:

At lunch time Hamid was picking up papers to keep the lawn area clean.

When Jane fell over, Maria helped her.

Provide simple but welcome incentives to those students whose names appear in the space.

Learning space

Divide part of the board into a number of spaces, each part to be used by a class group. In spare moments, members of the group add to a predetermined topic on the board.

For example: Words that include **bb**.

At the end of each week, the group with the most words is the winner. One group cannot copy the words of another group.

Spelling race hop

Divide the class into two lines. The lines stand facing the board roughly 3 metres from it. Call out a word to be spelt on the board. Calling out the word is the signal for the first two students to hop to the board, write the word on it and hop back to the end of their respective lines.

The next spelling word is called out and the next two students repeat the process. The line with the most words spelt correctly wins.

The same activity can be used to revise or reinforce maths and other factual subjects.

Joke of the week

Encourage student to bring their favourite short jokes or riddles to school and to write a bit of the joke on the board each day. 'Knock knock' jokes are suitable for this.

5 MINUTES

Cats and dogs

This variation of noughts and crosses can be played with spelling, maths and studies facts.

Draw a grid on the board. Divide the class into 'cats' and 'dogs'. Give a student on the cats' side a spelling word. If the student spells the word correctly he or she can choose a square and draw a cat in it. Now it is the dogs' turn.

The winning team is the first one to have three symbols in a row.

10 MINUTES

Rhyme time

Similar to 'Learning space' on page 62. Provide spaces for groups to add words rhyming with a given word you have chosen. The group that has the most words at the end of the week is the winner.

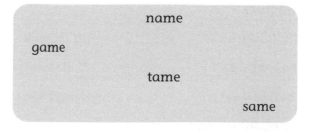

name

game

tame

same

5 MINUTES

Mystery object, mystery person

As for 'Mystery drawing' on page 61, have a mystery object or person described by one sentence each day.

For example:

Mon   I am a native African animal.

Tue   I have been known to attack humans.

Wed   I am smaller than an elephant.

Thurs   I am herbivorous and like to live in water.

Fri   I am sometimes called a 'river horse'.

Class members can guess at any time. However, someone who makes a guess on, for example, Tuesday cannot guess again that week. Write the guess and the name of the student on the board so their answer can be checked at the end of the week.

Board cricket

Prepare a spelling list relevant to all the students in the class.

Organise two teams:

* the bowlers who 'throw' (ask) the words to be spelt.

* the batters who must 'bat' these words back by spelling them correctly and so earn runs for their side.

The first batter comes forward.

The bowler 'throws' the first word from the list, such as 'village'. The batter replies, 'v–i–l–l–a–g–e'. This batter has scored one run.

For each correct response given, the batter scores one run. An incorrect response means he or she is out. The batting side that scores the most runs is the winner.

Maths and other facts can also be used.

Batters

Jin Jin ~~IIII~~ I = 6	Jin Jin spelt six words correctly
Paul III = 3	Paul spelt three words correctly
Hamid 0 = 0	Hamid spelt the first word incorrectly
Serap ~~IIII IIII IIII IIII IIII~~ = 25	Serap spelt 25 words correctly and scored 25 runs for her side.

Day and month

Write the days of the week and the months of the year in different languages. Combine this with your school's Modern Foreign Language programme.

See examples on page 68.

Letter starters

In a space on the board, write the outline of a letter in large print. In their own time, students write words beginning with the letter within the letter shape.

Fast finishers' section

Leave a space on the board for the fast finishers.

This may include puzzles such as:

- a number puzzle

- a rebus

- a 'Who Am I?' puzzle.

Games

Tables spin

Write five numbers on the board. Choose five students ('bottles') to stand under these, facing the board. For example:

Other students in the class call out times tables facts that correspond with one of the numbers on the board. The student standing under the correct number spins around immediately.

Example:

5 × 6 – the student standing under the number 30 must spin around immediately.

If the student fails to do so, he or she is replaced by another member of the class.

15 MINUTES

Number patterns relay

Write the start of some number patterns on the board.

Divide the class into teams, each team facing the board. At a given signal, the first player runs to the board and adds the next number in the pattern. He or she then passes the chalk to the next player in the team, who repeats the process. The activity continues until the pattern is finished. The first team to complete their pattern is the winner.

For example:

8, 13, 18 _ _ _ _ _ end

9, 16, 21 _ _ end

5 MINUTES

Word relays

Divide the class into equal relay teams, such as five groups of five members.

Write five initial blends on the board. (You can choose whether to keep these all the same or write four different blends.)

At a given signal, the first student in each team, all of which are facing the board, runs forward and writes a word beginning with the allocated blend. The student then hands the chalk to the next member of the team and returns to his or her seat. The next player writes a word in the same manner and so the process is repeated until all members of all teams are seated.

The first team to be seated wins.

For example:

Sh	Br	Tr	Ch	Fr
shop	bring	tray	chop	frog
shed		trust	chin	friend
		trick		fried
		try		

10 MINUTES

Thoughts for the week

Life is mainly froth and bubble,
Two things stand like stone:
Kindness in another's trouble,
Courage in your own.

There are two ways to get to the top of an oak tree: you can climb it or sit on an acorn.

Those who don't stand for something will fall for anything!

Knowledge will be distributed in this classroom, Monday to Friday.

Children are expected to bring their own containers.

Don't worry about school and no one will be any the wiser – especially you!

All my life I've been doubtful, but now I'm not so sure.

There are only six weeks between a bad haircut and a good one.

Success is not permanent. The same may also be said of failure.

Only boring people get bored.

Success is 10% inspiration and 90% perspiration!

If you see someone without a smile, give them yours.

If you have a poor memory don't worry, just forget all about it.

A bird in the hand is useless if you want to blow your nose!

Love your enemies; it will drive them crazy!

If it wasn't for venetian blinds it would be curtains for all of us!

Those who know and know not that they know are asleep – wake them!

Those who know and know that they know are wise – follow them!

Those who know not and know not that they know not are fools – shun them!

Those who know not and know that they know not are children – help them!

Days and months

French

Sunday	Monday	Tuesday	Wednesday	Thursday	Friday	Saturday
dimanche	lundi	mardi	mercredi	jeudi	vendredi	samedi

January	February	March	April	May	June
janvier	février	mars	avril	mai	juin

July	August	September	October	November	December
juillet	août	septembre	octobre	novembre	décembre

German

Sunday	Monday	Tuesday	Wednesday	Thursday	Friday	Saturday
Sonntag	Montag	Dienstag	Mittwoch	Donnerstag	Freitag	Samstag

January	February	March	April	May	June
Januar	Februar	März	April	Mai	Juni

July	August	September	October	November	December
Juli	August	September	Oktober	November	Dezember

Italian

Sunday	Monday	Tuesday	Wednesday	Thursday	Friday	Saturday
domenica	lunedi	martedi	mercoledi	giovedi	venerdi	sabato

January	February	March	April	May	June
gennaio	febbraio	marzo	aprile	maggio	giugno

July	August	September	October	November	December
luglio	agosto	settembre	ottobre	novembre	dicembre

Spanish

Sunday	Monday	Tuesday	Wednesday	Thursday	Friday	Saturday
domingo	lunes	martes	miércoles	jueves	viernes	sábado

January	February	March	April	May	June
enero	febrero	marzo	abril	maio	junio

July	August	September	October	November	December
julio	agosto	septiembre	octubre	noviembre	diciembre

Japanese

Sunday	Monday	Tuesday	Wednesday	Thursday	Friday	Saturday
nichi-yobi	getsu-yobi	ka-yobi	sui-yobi	moku-yobi	kin-yobi	do-yobi

January	February	March	April	May	June
ichi-gatsu	ni-gatsu	san-gatsu	shi-gatsu	go-gatsu	roku-gatsu

July	August	September	October	November	December
shichi-gatsu	hachi-gatsu	ku-gatsu	ju-gatsu	juichi-gatsu	juni-gatsu

Tips and Ideas to Encourage Student Participation

TO THE TEACHER

The following are tips and ideas for encouraging student participation. None of them requires a great deal of effort and most are based on common sense.

It is important on your first day with a new class to avoid the tough approach that gives the message: 'I'm not here to be liked, I'm here to teach.' While some people may think this approach sets you up as a person who means business, it can easily backfire. A student's first impressions of a teacher are important. In general, students will participate more actively and enthusiastically when they are being taught by teachers they like and respect.

Attainable goals

Set the students attainable goals.

The students will willingly participate in learning tasks that have an inherent interest and enjoyment and that allow them to acquire new skills and new knowledge. They are unlikely to participate in a task unless they think they stand a good chance of succeeding in it.

Success

Ensure that the students experience success.

There is a saying: 'Nothing succeeds like success!' Once students have successfully accomplished a task, they will be more likely to take risks in the future and participate in activities that are more challenging.

Accept mistakes

Encourage the students to accept that mistakes are an essential part of learning. Show them that we all learn by our mistakes. Use the board to remind them – write clearly in a permanent place on the board: 'Mistakes are an essential part of learning.'

Explain to them the adage: 'Show me a person who has never made a mistake and I'll show you someone who has never learnt anything.'

Students who are being taught in a supportive, non-threatening environment will participate willingly in all activities in the knowledge that they will not be ridiculed if and when they falter.

Participate with students

Be prepared to participate in student-organised activities.

Sometimes students organise plays, games and so on and they may need your assistance, participation or support. Be prepared to give it. Your participation in their activities will make them more willing to participate in your learning activities.

Carefully plan work tasks

Think extremely carefully before setting a work task.

Providing successful experiences to ensure full class participation is more difficult than it first appears.

Organise work tasks so that activities and exercises are based on what individual students have succeeded at in the past. Ensure that a large part of the content in every learning activity is at a level that can be completed by lower ability students without too much difficulty. Pitch only a small part of the content at a level that will challenge the ability of the most capable students. This will encourage all students to participate willingly in prescribed learning tasks.

The enjoyment of participation

Conduct plenty of challenging activities in which there are no winners, but simply the enjoyment of participation.

For example:

'Orange Baby' Week

Each student is given an orange to look after for the week. They must take their orange into the playground at break and lunch times and ensure no harm comes to it. In class the oranges are placed in a communal box. Each student must be able to recognise his or her particular orange. They take their orange home and return with it each day.

Such activities are non-threatening and, because there is no direct competition, students enjoy the fun of participating.

This activity fosters participation rather than competition.

Small group activities

Ensure you provide opportunities for each student to take part in small group activities. The student who is reluctant to participate with the whole class may feel more confident when taking part in small group or pair activities.

For example: Blindfold Day

One student is blindfolded and paired with a 'carer'. The carer must look after the 'blind'

student's welfare for the day (or part of the day) – guiding them to a seat, guiding and helping them get their lunch and so on.

Such cooperative activities encourage students to participate in broader class activities.

'Mighty things from small beginnings grow.'

John Dryden

Class resource book

Develop a class resource book. You could call it 'Our Yellow Pages'.

In the book, list the students and their particular skills and talents. Do not confine this to academic achievement only. Ensure

every student is listed and every talent, no matter how small, is recorded.

Encourage the class members to use other students as a resource of information and other skills.

Value contribution

When a student who is usually reluctant to participate does so, and achieves even a modest amount of success, ensure you make

a point of praising the student and telling him or her how valued this contribution has been.

Pairs

Don't rush reluctant participants into group project situations. Instead, start small. Use study partners and gradually build up the

size of groups. The reluctant participant will usually enjoy working with a partner who can act as an assistant and guide.

Interesting presentation

A student's reluctance to participate may simply reflect boredom or disinterest in the subject or its presentation.

Ask the students to mime or role play the lives of people they are studying. This will create a more vivid picture in the minds of the students than setting them to write copious notes.

Role play, puppets, models, guest speakers, teaching aids and so on will all encourage student interest and participation in various learning areas.

Present lessons in an interesting way.

Concentration break

Sometimes students fail to participate because they are tired and their interest is waning. It has been claimed that youngsters can only concentrate on a particulate topic for one to one-and-a-half minutes for every year of their age.

To encourage student participation, work at a concentrated activity with a older students for 20 to 30 minutes and then have a three- to five-minute break. During the break, conduct a 'thinking' activity or a dictionary game or similar. This short break will help to refresh students and they will usually return to the task with renewed enthusiasm and vigour.

Students in control

Spend time assisting reluctant participants to develop strategies to take control of their own learning and thinking processes. Assist them to set goals, evaluate their task performance and monitor their general progress.

To achieve this, help these students to set themselves realistic and specific goals.

For example:

'*To learn a group of ten words and make no more than two errors when I am tested.*'

This is a far more realistic goal than, say: '*To be the top speller in the year by the end of this term.*'

Common sense

Low-achieving students are usually reluctant participants because their lack of knowledge of basic concepts and prerequisite skills is readily detected by peers.

You can assist these students by using some common-sense approaches.

For example:

- Avoid placing these students in situations of failure. Do not ask them questions about work that you know they have no hope of answering.

- When teaching basic concepts and other subject matter, simplify the material and present it in small steps.

- Support achievements, no matter how small, with positive reinforcement to assist the development of self-esteem.

Purposeful activities

Ensure that the students can see a purpose for the academic tasks you provide. Even low achievers and reluctant participants will readily join in activities they see as purposeful and relevant.

For example:

If you are teaching students how to write a letter, arrange for them to write and post a real letter to someone from whom they will receive a reply.

Playground pal

If some students are reluctant to participate in activities at break times and prefer to play alone, ask one of the more outgoing students in the class to become a 'playground pal'. A bit of gentle assistance from a well respected member of the class may be the impetus needed for the shy student to join in break- and lunchtime activities.

Talk with reluctant students

If a student is reluctant to participate in academic or general class activities, take the time to sit down and discuss your observations in a non-intrusive, non-threatening way. The student may harbour some fear or concern that you can assist with.

Don't pressure him or her to tell you but, if they willingly wish to talk with you, be a good listener, and be prepared to discuss constructive strategies to overcome the problem.

Cooperation

Use every opportunity to stress cooperation among students to achieve common learning goals. Reluctant participants are more likely to join in activities where cooperative learning is taking place than those in which students are set against each other in a competitive way.

'Government and cooperation are in all things laws of life; anarchy and competition the laws of death.'

John Ruskin

Rewards

Use popular classroom activities as rewards for the less desirable learning activities.

By carefully observing students' preferred activities, you will be able to decide which are appropriate rewards.

For example:

'Those who improve their performance in subtraction today get five minutes on the computer.'

Praise

Constantly praise students and offer encouragement both at an individual and at class level. Avoid the use of meaningless reinforcers such as 'good' and 'nice'. Instead, make your praise a positive and effective reinforcement of improved work or attitude.

For example:

'Grace, your handwriting has improved so much I can really enjoy the report you have written!'

Continuous reinforcement

Use continuous reinforcement and encouragement during the early stages of learning new subject matter. This continuous reinforcement will motivate students to persist in the task until the new learning has become established.

Ability tasking

When assigning students to a group for research or project studies, ensure that each student has been given a specific task well within the range of his or her individual ability. In this way, each student will feel needed and that his or her part in the group is valued.

Capitalise on the subject

Capitalise on the intrinsic qualities of a subject by planning academic activities that the students will participate in because they are interested in the content or enjoy the activity. Provide the students with opportunities to respond actively and in a variety of ways, instead of just by listening or reading.

For example, students could:

- draw a diagram or picture.
- present a play or mime.
- use tactile experiences.

Recognise, acknowledge and appreciate students' efforts.

Display achievements

Where appropriate, display the students' achievements. The students always respond positively to such displays and will participate enthusiastically in tasks because a display of their work indicates recognition, acknowledgment and appreciation of their efforts.

Ten Tips on How to Form Groups

TO THE TEACHER

Throughout the normal school day there will be times when you want the students to form groups for a classroom game or activity, or an outdoor physical education activity.

Formal groups

If you are replacing the classroom teacher, you will probably find that there are permanent groups set up by the teacher; for example, 'Beetles', 'Butterflies', 'Moths' and so on, referring to reading groups or number groups. The students will be well aware of these.

If you are filling in a casual vacancy and there is no information left by the teacher concerning the various subjects in which students work together in groups, then seek this information from the students themselves. They are sure to tell you how each group operates and where materials and resources are kept.

If the classroom teacher you are replacing has a formal grouping system in place, don't alter it or allow students to alter it. There will most likely be a well thought out reason for the particular groupings and if you alter these you are undermining the judgement and authority of the class teacher.

Informal groups

There are lots of times when you want students to arrange themselves in groups or pairs quickly and with as little fuss as possible. The following are some tips for both casual and class teachers on how to help students form informal groups.

Clumps

To form small groups for physical education activities, play 'Clumps'.

Ask the students to move around freely.

When you are ready, call out a number; for example, 'Four!'

Students must quickly form groups of four and sit down.

Now you have your groups ready for the activity you have prepared.

Students who are unable to form a group of four because they were too slow can easily be added to existing groups.

This is also a good warm-up activity.

Lining up quietly outside the classroom

Phrase the request as a challenge rather than an order.

Don't say: 'Get into a straight line behind Ellie!'

Say: 'I wonder who will be the quietest and quickest to get into a straight line behind Ellie?'

Forming a circle

Phrase the request as a challenge rather than as an order.

Say: 'I wonder how long it will take you to all join hands – from now?'

Once students have joined hands it is easy to move them back two, three or four paces to form a circle.

Say: 'Now that was a good effort. I wonder who can drop their hands and walk back four paces so everyone is in a circle?'

Seven other ideas

Here are seven more ideas for requests and games that will help students to form groups.

Requests:

1 'Find others who have the same eye colour as you.'

2 'Find another person who has a birthday in the same month as you.'

3 'Find someone who reads the same books as you.'

4 'Find someone who has the same pen as you.'

Games:

1 Have students write their initials on a piece of paper. Draw the pieces out of a hat or box, pairing or grouping as you go.

2 Fill a box with coloured tiles. Ask the students to come out and reach high into the box to pull out a tile. Group together all the students who draw out the same colour tile.

3 Ask the students to write their name on a small piece of card on the back of which is some 'Blu tac'. Have them close their eyes and stick their card on the board. Their partner is the person whose name is on the card closest to theirs.

Assigning Student Roles and Cooperative Rule Making

In the beginning

At the beginning of the school year explain to the students that you need to ensure that the classroom runs smoothly. Discuss with the students the importance of sharing tasks.

Have the students form groups of three or four and ask them to brainstorm the tasks that will need to be done each day. Make a list of these on the board.

Ask the students to nominate either themselves or someone they know for the various tasks. Discuss with the class the importance of being reliable and responsible in the various roles.

The importance of cooperation

The activities below will help the students understand the importance of cooperation in sharing classroom roles:

- Ask the younger students to colour in together a very detailed drawing.

- Ask the older students to create a design for a classroom mural.

When students are finished, have them sit in a circle. Ask them to discuss whether the experience was successful and whether everyone shared the task equally.

Ask:

- 'How does it make you feel if someone does not do their share?'

- 'How do you feel if someone wants to do it all?'

- 'What happens when someone lets the team down?'

Variety of experiences

Provide the students with a variety of theoretical and real experiences in which they develop cooperative skills.

For example, ask the students to form groups of five. Give them time to discuss and then role play the following situation:

'You are on an excursion to the zoo. Your teacher has told you that you must stay in your group. Two of the group want to see the giraffes while the other three want to go to the other side to see the butterfly enclosure. If you wanted to do exactly as you've been asked by your teacher, what might you say to the others?'

Various roles

With the students, decide on the roles of responsibility your classroom needs. These roles may vary and the people responsible may change from day to day, or week to week. For younger students, phrase the roles in novel terms.

Some ideas include:

- **Gofer** – a student selected to run special errands for the teacher.

- **Board Cleaner** – a student who is responsible for cleaning the board and dusters.

- **Tidy Team** – students responsible for ensuring that all members of the class have cleared the floor of paper and for emptying the bins.

- **Greenies** – students assigned to water plants and to make sure the classroom is neat before leaving on a Friday.

- **Welcoming Committee** – a group of students responsible for ensuring a newcomer to the class knows where the toilets are, the times and places to eat lunch, particular school rules and so on.

With the students' input, decide how often the roles should change. When you have agreed, draw up a rota together. Ensure that every student has a turn at each role.

Contracts

To add to the sense of responsibility, ask the students to sign a contract for the week or term.

Praise and reward

Ensure that the students are aware that you take these rules seriously and appreciate their efforts. Be quick to praise students who have accepted their responsibilities and carried out their roles thoroughly.

Develop a reward scheme for jobs done well; for example, ten minutes extra on the computer and so on. Alternatively, present certificates to good helpers.

See photocopiable resource on page 87.

Giraffe chart

This is a variation on the 'star chart'. Using the photocopiable resource on page 88, make a copy for each student. Write each student's name next to their giraffe. When the students have completed the set tasks responsibly and successfully, they colour in one of the circles.

The role of referee

In PE, some students may be assigned the role of referee. It is important that all other students respect and understand the difficulty of this role. Classroom activities such as the one below will foster this understanding.

Ask the students to form groups of four or five. Ask each group to choose a coordinator. This student's role is to help the group make a decision.

However, the coordinator does not make the decision. Ask the group to arrive at a decision about one of the topics below:

- the sport we'd like to play next Friday
- a fundraising activity for the class
- the subject of a class play.

Contract certificates to good helpers

Presented to ....

for ....

THANK YOU
from all of us!

Date .... Signed ....

Class teacher

Contract

I ....

agree to ....

If I can't, I will ask someone else to do it.

Signed .... Witnessed ....

Class teacher

Giraffe

NAME: ....

DEVELOPING RULES

Clear rules that are well thought out act as signposts in promoting positive behaviour. Your role is to assist in the development of the rules and to explain and enforce those created.

However, for any classroom rules to be effective they need to have been developed through discussion and with input from the students.

This should occur early in the school year when you, as the teacher, have established your credibility among the students and they are aware of your leadership style. Involving students in the process of developing rules sends a clear message that their ideas, thoughts and contributions are valued by you.

The following are some things to consider and steps to follow when developing rules with students.

General approach

Rules should be phrased in positive terms rather than as orders.

For example: *'In our classroom we take turns to answer questions'* is better than *'Don't call out!'*

Do not have too many rules. This creates confusion and sometimes the students, and even the teacher, cannot remember them all.

Make sure the rules are clear and specific.

Rules should specify what is and is not acceptable behaviour.

For example: *'We talk quietly at our desks so we do not interrupt others.'*

When teaching rules to younger students, use mime, role play and similar activities.

All rules should be revised and discussed regularly.

Discuss with the students the need to have rules to protect the rights of all and to govern the way they work together in a non-threatening, secure environment.

Emphasise that any rules they suggest must be simple, clear and specific.

Mention also that there is no need to have lots of rules – they can just have the ones that they feel are important.

Ask the students also to consider 'understood consequences' for significant infringements of others' rights.

Discuss the meaning of rights. Reiterate that, although we have individual rights, this also entails certain responsibilities.

Discuss, for example, the fact that everyone has the right to their say providing that they have their say fairly and give the same courtesy to others.

At the end of the class discussion, ask the students to form groups to develop rules they feel are essential to their class.

Give them 10 to 15 minutes for this discussion.

Student rules

The students should be encouraged to write the rules using their own language. They should include rules which relate specifically to:

1 **Conflict settlement** – solving classroom disputes in a manner acceptable to all parties.

2 **Communication** – covering areas such as yelling out, interrupting, teasing, racist and other hurtful remarks.

3 **Movement** – specifying the amount and kind of movement acceptable to all. It might also mention appropriate permission for leaving the room and the courtesy of letting the teacher (you) know your whereabouts at all times.

4 **Property** – mentioning such things as the right to be able to bring possessions to school without fear of them being damaged or stolen.

5 **Safety** – covering safe behaviour in certain activities such as cooking, art, physical education, sport and so on. It may also mention bringing dangerous toys or weapons to school or wearing unsafe clothing or jewellery that the class as a whole deems as unacceptable and inappropriate.

6 **Routines and duties** – covering the sharing of classroom duties and the manner in which these duties should be carried out.

For example: *cleaning the blackboard, canteen duty, packing up* and so on.

7 **Learning times** – covering learning situations, how to get the teacher's (your) attention or assistance during work times times, taking turns at work stations, using the computer, early finishing and coming into the classroom prepared – bringing appropriate equipment.

8 **Togetherness** – covering the feelings that students have for each other. It means not denigrating people because they are slow learners or quick learners, have physical disabilities, look different or come from different backgrounds and so on.

9 **Consequences** – students should suggest fair and acceptable consequences for those who break the rules. These may include exclusion from certain activities, replacing damaged property, working in isolation, staying behind or withdrawal of certain privileges. Remember, you must enforce any consequences and the students will expect you to do so. If you fail to, the whole exercise of cooperative rule making may well be a waste of time.

Making rules work

Call the students back together

At the end of the group session, call the students back together. Have each group's spokesperson present their rules. Write all the rules on the board or on large sheets of paper.

Careful consideration

Encourage the students to consider carefully all the rules and consequences presented. Students should remove those rules that the majority feel are not necessary or are worded inappropriately. If agreement cannot be reached on a particular rule, you may have to arbitrate and make the final decision.

Record the rules

Make a printed copy of the rules when everyone (including yourself) is satisfied that those chosen are fair and uphold the fundamental values of honesty, cooperation, caring, tolerance and personal responsibility.

Distribute a copy to each student to attach to their table or paste in an exercise book.

Alternatively, make a large copy that can be displayed in an appropriate part of the classroom.

Revise rules

From time to time, revise the rules with your students. Ask them if they still feel that all the rules and consequences they developed are relevant. Should any be changed or modified in the present circumstances?

Quiet rule reminders

A good deal of discipline may include quiet rule reminders. For this reason, rules should be regularly referred to and enforced. However, if the rules have been developed cooperatively by students, compliance is more likely to occur.

Class Assembly Ideas

TO THE TEACHER

Class assemblies provide a great opportunity to foster a sense of togetherness among students. They can be a time for planning the week or for talking about past events. They can be:

- times for rewarding those who deserve it, and times to mention the achievements of classmates.

- times when individual students can share their concerns or worries with others – a time for caring, sharing and helping.

- a learning time or simply a time to enjoy some activities as a group.

Item time

Encourage the students to present an item to the rest of the class during assembly time. It may be a joke or poem they have made up, a song they would like to sing, a piece of group miming and so on. Such activities, when they are appreciated without criticism, foster the development of self-esteem and a caring environment.

Share time

During class assemblies encourage the students to show others their favourite possessions. Encourage them to explain why it is their favourite possession and why it is special to them.

Visiting speakers

Class assembly time provides a great opportunity for visiting speakers to address students. For example: 'Occupation Time'.

Invite local tradespeople and professionals to talk for 5 to 10 minutes about their occupations. For example, over a period of four weeks arrange talks by a police officer, a mechanic, a pharmacist and a lawyer. Your parent group may be able to help out with this.

Alternatively, you could ask local entertainers and musicians to speak to the class and demonstrate their skills; for example, a magician, pianist, ventriloquist and so on.

Getting to know you

Class assembly time creates a great opportunity to get to know your students better.

Allow the students time to reflect on their lives and everyday activities and encourage them to share their thoughts with you. Let them tell you about their interest, hobbies, family and so on.

Class projects

Use class assembly time to encourage the students to organise and discuss whole-class projects. These could include:

- a school playground clean up campaign (all levels).

- planning visits to an elderly people's home (older students).

- possible guest speakers to invite (all levels)

- planning a party for the local Day Care children (older students).

My worries

Use class assembly times to allow the students the opportunity to express any worries or concerns they may have. Other students may be able to assist.

For example: *'Yesterday I lost my best marble in the playground. It was my favourite and I'd love to get it back.'*

Create a new room display

Use class assembly times to create a new room display or to decorate the room for a particular theme you are presently engaged in. For example:

- In March, decorate the room for the Spring Equinox.

- At the end of October decorate the classroom for Halloween.

Positive clumps

Ask the students to move around freely.

When you are ready, call out a number; for example, 'Two!'

The students must quickly form groups of two and sit down.

Now both students are expected to say one positive thing about their partner.

- *'My partner Sion has a happy smile.'*
- *'My partner Billy can do tricks on his bicycle.'*

On a signal, students move around again until you call out 'Two'. Repeat the process.

Noughts and crosses

Draw a noughts and crosses grid on the board and write the names of nine students in the spaces.

Select two students to play each other. They may face the board or the class*, whichever way you wish to play the game. One plays for noughts and one for crosses.

They select the name of a student from the grid and are asked a question about that student.

For example: *'Paul.'* – *'Where does Paul live?'*

For a correct answer a nought or cross is put in the space corresponding with Paul's name. The first with three in a row wins.

*For older students to play facing away from the board, have players describe the space they want by saying 'top right', 'middle left', 'bottom middle' and so on.

Tags

Ask students to write their name on a small piece of paper. Place these in a small box. Choose a player to draw a name from the box and read it out; for example: 'Maria'.

Another selected student asks the player a question about Maria.

For example: *'What colour eyes does Maria have?'*

If the player answers correctly, he or she then draws another name out and the process is repeated. If he or she fails to answer the question correctly, the student to whom the question referred becomes the player.

Award time

Use class assemblies as a time to reward students for achievements.

Certificates can easily be photocopied. There may be an 'Improvement Award' or 'Congratulations for Being Such a Kind Class Helper' and so on.

Some students may wish to present one of these awards to other members of the class. Encourage the students to nominate recipients by asking them if someone in the class has done something special for them or others.

For example: *'Today at lunchtime Sally helped me learn my spelling so I think she should be considered next assembly for a Caring Classmate Award.'*

See photocopiable resource on page 98.

School helper

In class assembly time, encourage the students to express their observations of the positive actions of others in the class. Knowing these actions are seen and appreciated by class members helps students develop more positive attitudes.

For example: *'Last Tuesday Michael and Susan helped the headteacher clean up the bike shed.'*

'This morning I saw Paul showing four-year-olds how to play a game.'

See photocopiable resource on page 98.

Class rewards

Class assemblies provide a great opportunity to reward the whole class for special achievements.

For example:

- keeping a section of the playground tidy for a week.

- everyone doing their homework.

- keeping the corridor or bag storage area tidy and so on.

See photocopiable resource on page 98.

Improvement Award

Class ....

congratulates

....

for fantastic improvement in

....

Well done from all of us!

Nominated by: ....

Caring Classmate Award

Class ....

congratulates

....

for being such a kind class helper!

Thank you from all of us!

Nominated by: ....

School Helper Award

Class ....

thanks

....

for being such a great school helper when you

....

....

Thank you from all of us!

Nominated by: ....

Whole Class Reward

Thank you to Class

....

for

....

....

Your reward is

....

Signed ....

Activities that Involve 2, 3 and 4 Year Groups

TO THE TEACHER

There are times when general or specific activities involve more than one year. This might be because a number of years wish to work together on a common academic or social service project; because of streaming students in learning areas; or to combine resources for a particular learning area.

Another valuable reason for combining years is to provide opportunities for social interaction among students of different age groups. This may take the form of assisting with school work or simply a relaxed afternoon of playing games together.

When organising mixed year physical games, ensure that the students are not handicapped by their age, sex or strength. Choose or modify activities so all will have an equal opportunity to experience success.

Projects

Join with other years to work together on a specific project.

For example:

- cleaning up the local school environment.
- planting trees at a nearby reserve.
- visiting a home for the elderly or day care centre to talk to the people there.
- considering ways to raise money for a special humanitarian project.

There are dozens of other projects that can be approached in this way.

Topics – working together

Choose a topic from an academic area and arrange for students of different years to work on activities together at various levels of difficulty. A mixed ability/age group works well here, as the different students will have different strengths, interests and experiences to share with each other.

Have students work in small groups.

Organise activities so that all members of the group can work through a set number of activities at the lowest level. They can then choose activities at any other level.

Ask older students to assist the younger ones by showing them how to research and develop the chosen topic. This gives all students the opportunity to be extended and to think creatively, critically and analytically.

Try this approach in various academic areas.

Sing-alongs

From time to time, join two or more years together for a sing-along. Photocopy words to songs, and pair older with younger students to help with the reading. Use taped music or instrumental accompaniment if you or a colleague can play.

Students may also wish to move to the beat of the music. Most younger students remember words better if combined with movements.

This kind of activity may be formalised into a regular singing or choral group.

Plays and fairy tales

A performance combining all the years is a great way of bringing classes together and can be performed for parents at the end of the year.

Choose roles according to the age and ability of the students.

For example, in 'Snow White' younger students can play the animals and dwarfs while older students play Snow White, the King, Queen, Prince Charming and so on. With all the activities involved in staging such an event, there are opportunities for every class to be involved both on stage and behind the scenes.

Alternatively, form groups of similar aged students and challenge each group to present their version of a fairy tale, nursery rhyme, legend and so on.

Reading buddies

Arrange for older students to listen to young ones read. Apart from assisting young students to develop reading skills, this activity also helps older students gain reading practice (especially those who may struggle a little) and gives them a chance to develop qualities of patience and care.

Games time

Every so often, meet with another year to have 'games time' involving various quizzes; for example: tables quizzes, spelling quizzes and so on.

Finish the picture

Ask each student in your class to begin a picture on a sheet of paper. Stop them before they complete their drawings. While your students are doing this, arrange for students in a colleague's class to do the same.

Swap the unfinished pictures between the years so that the drawings are completed by the other year.

It doesn't matter if you swap pictures with a higher or lower year than yours.

When the pictures are completed and handed back, ask the students to comment on the now completed picture. Was this what they had in mind when they started?

Yellow Pages

Provide the students with a sheet of paper and ask them to list all the things they are good at or know a lot about. On the other side have them make a short list of things they sometimes have trouble with or would like to be able to do better. Collect the sheets and collate all the material.

Ask teachers from other years to do the same.

In this way you can build up a valuable bank of information of students who would be suitable to help others in lots of various areas. These 'helpers' may be in any year.

Think tanks

Join with other years on a regular basis to form 'think tanks' to solve problems arising at school.

For example: '*The school playground is becoming messier and messier. What are some ways to prevent this?*'

It is best if students from a number of years are able to discuss such problems together rather than leaving it to one year only. This is the basis of active Student Representative Councils.

Make sure that constructive suggestions are acknowledged and acted upon.

Challenges

Group students together from two or more years and provide them with challenges in which they all must have input.

For example:

- Provide each group with 20 straws and a roll of tape and challenge them to make a tower which can support the weight of a cloth or pencil at the greatest possible height above its base.

- Provide a mixed group of students with a box of matches and a roll of tape. Challenge them to make a structure that leans out as far as possible from the side of a table without collapsing.

- Challenge the group to build a tower using only a box of matches and some Blu tak.

Murals

Combine with another year or years to paint a mural together. Select a venue, such as a corridor, along which the mural can stretch.

Have the students from all the years meet to plan the materials, theme and so on.

A great way to brighten a dull corridor!

Chocolate race

Wrap chocolate bars with numerous layers of newspaper, sealing each layer with tape (as in 'Pass the Parcel').

Divide the students into groups and give each group a die. On the signal, students in each group take it in turns to roll the die. The first to throw a six begins removing one sheet of paper from the parcel. The other groups continue throwing their die and as soon as another six is thrown that group takes over the unwrapping.

Each sheet of paper must be completely removed before 'attacking' the next. The group that gets to the chocolate first, wins it!

To make it more interesting, have the students use a fork or two rulers to remove the sheets!

A fun activity for the last day of term.

Posters

Provide the students with appropriately sized drawing paper. Have them design and illustrate a poster. Make the topics positive social builders. For example:

- An anti-bullying poster.

- How we can help others?

- Ways to stop littering the school grounds.

A good community spirit builder!

Same as

This is an activity that helps students from different years to get to know each other. In conjunction with other teachers, prepare a sheet similar to the one below and give one to each student.

Outside, encourage students to mix freely. Ask them to find someone who matches them in a particular category; for example,

favourite food, eye colour and so on. Ask them to list the names of these students on the right-hand side. They may match any one thing with more than one student.

Encourage the students not only to write down and match the names but also to discuss why they may like the same football team and so on.

Favourite football team: **Manchester United**	**Sally, Joel, Mike, Hamid**
Eye colour: **Brown**	**Joel, Tom, Jin Jin**
Hair colour: **Black**	**Mia, Jin Jin, Hamid**
Type of pet I own: **Dog**	**Jack, Jake, Mia**
Favourite food: **Pizza**	**Tina, Charles**
Favourite sport: **10-Pin Bowling**	**Jin Jin, Mike**
Favourite band: **Stereophonics**	**Joel**

A great way to encourage all school members to get to know each other!

Group sports

Divide the students into groups of equal numbers from different years.

Choose activities that they are all able to do competently; for example: throwing a ball into a bin. Stand older students further back for their turn.

When the activity has been completed by all the groups, award points to the group that moves the quickest and quietest to the next activity.

Alternatively, play taped music to signal the move to the next activity and award points to the group that moves in the most rhythmic way.

Spin the bottle

Assemble students from three or four years in the playground. Divide the playground into four sections. (You can use chalk to do this.) Play taped music and ask the students to move to the music in any direction. When the music stops, walk to the centre and spin a bottle. The students who are in the section the bottle is pointing to when it stops are out. Keep going until one person is the winner.

Jump the broom

A broom (or brooms) is laid down and when the music is played students run, hop or skip over it. Students move in a circle. The last student to have jumped over the broom when the music stops is out.

Paper stands

Lay sheets of newspaper around the playground. Play taped music while the students run around, avoiding the sheets. When the music stops, each student stands on a sheet of paper. No part of their feet should be showing over the edge of the paper. If so, they are out.

After each turn, fold the sheets of paper in half so they progressively become smaller and more difficult to stand on. Smaller students will find this easier than larger students!

Hokey Cokey

The 'Hokey Cokey' is a movement activity thoroughly enjoyed by students of all ages. It lends itself to participation by a number of years. Most schools should have tapes of these and other dances available.

Balloon pats

Arrange students in groups from different years. Give each group member a number and ask the group to form a circle. Toss a balloon into the centre of each circle and when the teacher or the group leader calls their number that player must give the balloon a pat to keep it in the air. If the balloon drops to the ground, the player whose responsibility it was to pat it up is out.

The leader will have to remember the numbers of the remaining players, so re-number the players every so often, beginning with 1.

A great group cooperation activity!

Against the wall

Combine with another class and ask the students to form small groups. Give each member of the group a number. Each group should have a quoit, frisbee or another suitable throwing object.

Call out a number, such as 'three'. Each 'three' must come out and stand on a line. They then toss the quoit, trying to get it closest to the wall (or a predetermined line). When all 'threes' have had their go, the student whose quoit is the closest earns a point for his or her group.

Team teaching

You may at some stage wish to consider team teaching with one or more other years.

This sharing of teaching responsibilities may be with classes in the same year as yours or across years with teachers of various age groups pooling their skills and resources.

Essentials for team teaching

Try to commit yourself to team teaching with colleagues that you know will complement your style of teaching. Each team member must be tactful, punctual, able to listen and change if necessary, and cooperative.

Be prepared for extra demands on your time. You will have to get to know many more students and to consult frequently with other team members – especially if you wish to alter any aspect of the organisation.

Determine guidelines

Determine guidelines for team organisation. Together, agree to specific goals, organisational structure and the responsibilities of each team member. Also discuss the different philosophies of teaching that are bound to surface in these arrangements. Write up these guidelines so they can be signed off by the team members and referred to if needed. Throughout the term, meet to discuss progress and, if necessary, agree to modify or alter these guidelines.

Ensure courses of study are agreed to and followed. Only when you have structured the content of curriculum areas can you establish specific objectives and devise appropriate methods of evaluation.

All team members must be consistent regarding the rules set for students. It is best to involve the students when you devise team rules.

Ensure that forming two, three or more years into a team teaching structure will not interfere with the programmes of other staff members; for example: specialist timetables, annual excursions, sports days, and so on.

Some suggested forms of organisation

- As home teacher, stay with your year in the morning for English and maths. In the afternoon, arrange the classrooms for art, science, physical education and so on. The students choose what to work on.

- Leave the doors between the classrooms open. Each teacher instructs the combined class in different subject areas. When not engaged in direct teaching, the 'resting teacher' assists with corrections, evaluation and so on.

- Set up the room in subject or curriculum areas. Each teacher specialises in a particular subject and stays in that area all day. Groups of students rotate between these.

- Set up different learning areas around the different rooms. Timetable the students to move with their home teachers between subject areas.

- Provide individual students or groups of students with assignments outlining work to complete each day. The students may decide the order in which they do this. The teacher can be based in subject areas, look after their home group, or generally supervise all the students.

- Teachers with special talents in a learning area swap students for that subject. For example, one teacher may be good at teaching music, while another has a talent for teaching science. Arrange to swap classes for a set period so that students learn from the 'expert' teacher.

Activities for a Rainy Day

Calm Activities

Pop Art

You will need:

- a soft drink can

- a large piece of drawing paper for each student

- poster paints.

Place the can for all to view. Ask the students to draw the can, enlarged about eight or ten times. You may like to show them some Pop Art paintings as inspiration!

20 MINUTES

Fruit sculpture

You will need:

- an assortment of suitable fruit and vegetables (celery sticks, carrots, potatoes, radishes, olives, tomatoes, cucumbers, sultanas, apples)

- coloured toothpicks.

Allow the students to create a sculpture or creature of their own by sticking the fruits and vegetables together with toothpicks. Pieces of grass or parsley can be added for hair. The creatures can be eaten later!

40 MINUTES

Jigsaws

You will need:

- colourful magazines, outdated calendars and TV posters and so on

- a supply of cardboard

- glue or paste

- varnish or similar

- scissors.

Ask the students to find a suitable, colourful picture from the magazines and so on. Alternatively, students can paint their own colourful pictures directly onto the cardboard.

Glue the picture onto the cardboard. When it is dry, cover the picture with a protective coating of clear varnish.

The students now cut the picture into small pieces.

Ask the students to jumble the pieces and challenge another student to reassemble them.

When the activity is finished, ask each student to place the pieces in an envelope labelled with his or her name. You now have a ready supply of jigsaws for other rainy days.

40 MINUTES

Memory move

Arrange the class into groups of four or five. Tell each group to face one way and to move only when the teachers says 'move'.

The teacher then gives a number of orders which the students listen to and follow on the word 'Move'.

For example: 'Left turn, move.' 'Two paces forward, move.' 'Right turn, a pace backwards, and about turn, move.'

The winning group is the one who has the most students facing in the correct direction after carrying out all the moves.

20 MINUTES

Heads and tails

You will need:

- old newspapers and magazines

- paper

- glue or paste.

Provide the students with plenty of old newspapers and magazines. Ask them to search through these, cutting out the heads and bodies of people. They can then make collages sticking the heads randomly to bodies.

For example: a baby's head on an adult's body and so on.

40 MINUTES

Newspaper chase

Give each student a copy of the same newspaper (or a few pages photocopied). Alternatively, divide the class into teams.

Call out questions.

For example:

'What is the price of the Ford Focus from Honest Joe's on page 9?'

'What number would you telephone to find out about the lost dog on page 27?'

The first team with the correct answer scores a point. The team that scores the most points wins.

This exercise can also be done by providing the questions on a sheet of paper. The winner is the person or team with the most correct answers in the shortest time.

Leaf picture

Ask the students to bring a leaf into the classroom at the end of the lunch break. Ask students to paste the leaf onto some paper and draw a head, arms and feet with pastels or crayons.

Long leaves can be transformed into animals or birds.

Who am I? What am I?

This game challenges students to guess who a person is or what something is from given clues. With a little thought, clues can soon be created.

For example:

- I was created by Walt Disney. I am a type of bird. My initials are D.D. I have starred in many cartoons. Who am I?

- I am a shape. I have three sides and three angles. My names begins with 't'. What am I?

Clues can be made more difficult for older students.

Designs

Ask the students to design a machine and describe how it works.

For example:

- a new super mouse trap

- a super kennel for the modern dog that demands the very best of everything.

Itemising

You will need:

- a tray

- various items such as a pen, eraser, matchbox, counter, coin, scissors, paper clip and so on.

1 The students sit in a circle. Each has a pencil and piece of paper. Place the tray of objects in the middle of the circle. Allow the students to view the objects for one minute then remove or cover the tray. The students must write or draw all the objects they can remember.

2 Alternatively, hold up a number of the items for students to view. The students must not write until they have viewed all the objects. When you put down the last object, say 'Write'. Students must list each object in the order they were presented.

Vary the number of objects according to the age of the students.

Two great memory games!

Shaping up

You will need:

- photocopies of various shapes – triangles, squares, rectangles, circles and so on
- scissors
- a list of objects written on the board, such as a house, a boat, the sun, a wheel and so on.

Have students draw around each shape to create an object either chosen from a list on the board or of their own choice, then cut their object out.

Dead fish

The students find a space of their own on the floor and spread out in a starfish shape. They must not make even the slightest movement. Those who do are out!

Stand-up garden

You will need:

- paper
- coloured pencils
- pipe cleaners
- staplers.

Ask the students to draw and colour a flower garden as though they were in a tree looking down on it.

Next ask them to draw and cut out a butterfly, bird or bee.

Twist a pipe cleaner around a pencil to form a spring. Now ask students to staple the pipe cleaner to both the garden and the creature they have made.

Time out

You will need a watch with a second hand or a stopwatch.

Cover any clocks in the room so they cannot be seen by the students. The aim of the game is for students to judge accurately a set, predetermined time, such as one minute, half a minute and so on.

Ask students to stand. Say: 'We are going to judge one minute's time. When you think a minute is over, sit down. Starting from … now!' The student who sits down closest to the minute is the winner.

For an interesting variation, ask questions or talk to try to spoil their concentration.

An excellent estimation activity!

Finish the saying

Begin by starting a well-known saying.

For example: 'An apple a day…'

The students either say the ending or write it down (… keeps the doctor away).

Other examples include:

- A stitch in time (saves nine).
- The early bird (catches the worm).

Proverbs are good for this game.

Crazy options

You will need:

- old newspapers and magazines
- glue or paste.

Ask the students to search through the newspapers and magazines to find and cut out pictures of people or animals.

Ask them to paste these pictures on a sheet of paper and draw talking balloons from the mouths of the cut-outs. Now students can write in the balloons what they think the person or animal is saying. These can be as humorous as they please!

Still art

You will need:

- enough drawing paper for each student

- a piece of drawing charcoal or pencil for each student

- a still life – bowl of fruit or vase of flowers and so on.

Provide each student with a sheet of paper and a piece of charcoal. Set up the still life at the front of the room and ask students to sketch it.

You might like to start this activity by asking the students not to look at the paper but to follow the contour of the still life very slowly with their eyes and let their charcoal (their hand) follow those contours. This will assist them to really look a what they are drawing. Reassure them that it doesn't matter if at the end their drawing looks like scribble! They can spend 5 minutes doing this contour drawing.

They can then dust off the excess charcoal and touch up the drawing while looking at it.

40 MINUTES

Piecing it together

You will need some photocopied short stories or passages.

Ask the students to cut the passage into its various paragraphs so that each student has at least six strips of paper.

Next, give each student a sheet of paper. Ask them to paste the first paragraph of the passage at the top of this paper.

Now each student passes the paper, along with the other paragraph strips, to another student. That student reads the pasted-down paragraph plus the others and pastes the others in their correct order below the first paragraph.

For younger students, the first and last paragraphs may be pasted down.

30 MINUTES

Pocket my pride

Ask the students to empty their pockets, bag or desk and to arrange and draw the contents.

This activity provides a great opportunity to talk about design and layout.

40 MINUTES

Atlas search

You will need:

- atlases

- some prepared clues (see below).

Make up some confusing clues for towns and cities in a part of a country or for a country as a whole. Write these clues on the board and challenge the students to find the towns or cities.

For example: Male's Paddock (Mansfield), not yet used King's home (Newcastle), Holy Beatle (St Paul, George or John), my French friend (Miami), internal organ swimming facility (Liverpool).

15 MINUTES

Big words

Write a number of 'big' words on the board. Ask the students to study these and write what they think the words mean. Then ask the students to find the words in the dictionary and explain the actual definition. Were they correct?

Here are some to try: somnambulism, melancholy, diminutive, poltergeist, enraptured, meringue, menagerie, jettison, intermediary.

30 MINUTES

Sports think

Provide a list of tasks about various sports for students to complete.

Example:

1 Write down the names of all the sports you can think of that: are played with a ball; need bats, sticks or racquets; are played in water; or need an umpire or referee.

2 Make a list of all the board games you know.

3 Choose your favourite sport. Write the names of your ten favourite players, then draw a picture of the clothes they wear to play their sport.

20 MINUTES

Advertisements

Ask the students to write and illustrate their own advertisements.

For example:

● An advertisement for a pair of trainers as it might appear in a student magazine; then as it might appear in an adult magazine.

● An advertisement for a coming sporting event such as football finals, Olympic Games and so on.

● An invitation to listen to you, the expert, on how to make a great hamburger or pizza.

15 MINUTES

Making decisions

Create a situation which the students must discuss and make a decision on.

Look at the following scenario:

Imagine you and two friends are going camping in a tent near a lake. There are no shops or houses for over 50 kilometres.

From the following list of items, you can choose only six items between three of you:

Some chocolate bars, fishing lines, a length of strong rope, fishing bait, a pair of wellingtons, a large knife, pens and paper, comics to read, a first aid kit, sleeping bags, a box of matches and a compass.

Arrange the students into small groups. Allow them 15 minutes or more to reach a unanimous decision. Have them choose one person to be group leader to report on the decisions they have made at the end of the activity.

The above is only an example and, with a little thought, numerous situations such as this can be developed.

This is an excellent activity for older students!

30 MINUTES

Physical Activities

TO THE TEACHER

It's pouring with rain and you promised your students some physical activities. Don't despair. There are lots of physical activities for the classroom or gym. The only preparation needed is to move the furniture.

(Times given for each activity are minimum.)

Musical rocks

You will need pieces of cardboard – these are your 'rocks'. Place the cardboard on the floor around the room. On a signal, the students begin jogging around the room, taking care not to step on any of the 'rocks'. When the teacher calls 'Rocks!', everyone must stand on a piece of cardboard, making sure no part of their body is on the floor.

Students who cannot fit onto a 'rock' drop out of the game.

Remove one of the 'rocks' and resume jogging. The game progresses until one person is left.

 10 MINUTES

Noses to toeses

One student is the 'caller' and the rest of the class form into pairs. The caller nominates two different parts of the body such as 'elbows to ankles', 'toes to noses' or 'necks to waists'.

The paired players must then connect the parts of the body nominated with their

partners – as quickly as possible. They may sit or lie down when necessary.

This is great fun and requires a bit of thought and cooperation to achieve some positions.

 5 MINUTES

The hugging game

One player is the 'tagger'. The tagger's object is to catch a single person on the run. The only way for the other students to escape being tagged is to hug someone, in pairs or in a group of any number. As soon as the 'danger' is past, the hugs must be broken and players run freely again. Anyone caught becomes the next tagger.

Colour catch

The class stands in a circle with a selected student in the centre. The student in the centre names a colour and then a part of the body; for example: yellow/elbow.

Students move off, trying not to be tagged by the caller before putting that part of the body named on the colour stated. The colour can be found anywhere in the room. Players who are tagged drop out of the game.

Seeds to trees

This activity is improved with good music!

Ask the students to lie on the floor, curled up, and imagine they are the tiny seeds of a plant. Ask them to begin to grow and gradually unfold into a tree or a flower, miming the growth of a plant.

When this has been accomplished, ask them to imagine themselves as the plant living through each of the seasons. Ask them to mime how the plant is affected by the sun, rain, wind and perhaps snow, ending with spring.

Donkeys

You will need a blindfold. Select a player from among the students. The rest form a circle and walk around in a ring. Blindfold the player and stand him or her in the centre of the moving ring.

The player points towards the circle of students and says 'Bray like a donkey!'

The students moving in the ring immediately stop and the person who was pointed to pretends to be a donkey and brays at the player. If the player guesses who is braying, they change places and the game continues.

Lions and tigers

Arrange students in two lines, facing each other. One line is the 'lions' and the other the 'tigers'. You will also need to identify 'home' for each group.

The 'caller' (teacher or a class member) calls out 'Lion!' or 'Tiger!'

The group that has been named runs for 'home' and the opposition tries to tag them. Tagged children drop out of the game.

5 MINUTES

Cat and mouse

You will need two blindfolds.

Players sit in a large circle. Two are chosen to be the 'cat' and the 'mouse' respectively. They move into the circle and are blindfolded.

On a signal, the 'cat' tries to catch the 'mouse'. The 'mouse' claps occasionally to give the 'cat' clues to its position in the circle, then moves away quickly as the 'cat' tries to find it.

5 MINUTES

Music movements

You will need some lively music. Play the music and encourage the students to move freely to it. Tell them that when the music

stops they must 'freeze' and hold whatever position they are in until the music starts again.

5 MINUTES

Up and down

Divide the students into teams of four or five. The members of each team link arms sideways then sit down and stand up together, five times. Arms must stay linked at all times. The first team to finish – together – wins.

Chair sit

You will need a number of sturdy wooden-railed chairs and be sure that the chairs are strong enough for the activity.

Divide the class into groups of four or five. Each group is assigned one of the chairs.

On a signal, each group must try, in 20 seconds, to get all of its members off the ground and onto the chair. Any group that is unable to accomplish this is disqualified and the game continues.

A variation is to decrease the time allowed each time.

Horse races

You will need a number of blindfolds.

Pair together four to eight players. Each pair consists of a 'horse' and a 'jockey'. 'Horses' only are blindfolded.

The remaining students form a circle to act as a buffer. The 'horses' race around the circle with the 'jockeys' guiding them. Give them a target for finishing the race, such as completing two whole circuits.

Detectives

You will need a small object to hide.

Select a 'detective' and ask him or her to wait outside the room. Hide the selected object. When the 'detective' returns the rest of the class hums loudly to indicate closeness to the hidden object and softly to indicate distance from it. The 'detective's' turn ends when he or she finds the hidden object.

Ha ha ha

The aim of this game is not to laugh or show any expression of humour!

Students form a circle. A selected player begins the game by saying 'Ha ha ha'. The player on his or her right continues 'Ha ha ha' and so on.

Any player who actually laughs, grins or smiles or does not say the correct number of 'Ha's' is out.

5 MINUTES

Blow me down

You will need a low table and a ping pong ball.

The students kneel around the table with their hands clasped behind their backs.

Place the ping pong ball in the middle of the table. The aim is for students to blow the ball over the side of the table opposite to where they are kneeling and to prevent it from being blown over their side.

5 MINUTES

Circle ball

You will need a ball.

Pick two teams. One team (the scoring side) forms a circle. This team has the ball.

The members of the other team line up beside the circle and begin to run, one at a time, around the outside of the circle. The team with the ball must pass it around as quickly as possible, without dropping it. The object is to see how many times they can complete a circuit with the ball, before all the members from the other team have run around them.

Teams then change positions.

10 MINUTES

Paper relay

You will need 10 or 12 pieces of cardboard or A4 paper, folded over twice.

Students are divided into small relay teams of four or five.

The leader is given two pieces of cardboard or paper. The object is for the leader to move around the room, keeping his or her feet always on the pieces of the cardboard, and back to the next relay member who then does the same thing. The first team to successfully 'run' all its members in this manner wins.

7 MINUTES

Knotty problems

You will need two pieces of string, about one metre in length.

Students are divided into two teams. The leader of each team is given a piece of string.

On a given signal, the leader must tie a knot in the string, then pass it on to the next player who ties another knot and so on. The fastest team wins.

5 MINUTES

Hit the duster

You will need a duster and some chalk.

Students divide into two teams and line up on opposite sides of the room.

Two lines, about two metres apart, are marked on the floor and the duster is placed in the centre between these lines.

Students take off their shoes and begin throwing them at the duster.

The object is to move the duster over the other team's line. After throwing their own shoes, players may throw any shoes that fall near them.

Make it clear that the shoes are to be thrown at the duster only, and not at anything else!

Balloon ball

You will need two boxes and a balloon. (Keep some spare balloons to hand.)

Place a box at either end of the room. These are the goals.

Select two teams. The aim is for each team to get the balloon into their goal box.

Tapping the balloon is enough to get it moving.

Picks ups

You will need pencils or other small items.

Students stand with their heels against a wall and try to pick up a pencil placed a metre away. They must not lift their heels from the wall.

Opposites and similars

You will need a ball for this game.

The students form a circle with the teacher in the centre. The teacher calls out a word such as 'hot' and adds 'opposite or similar', and throws the ball to a student who must answer with a word that is opposite or similar, and throw the ball back.

If the student cannot answer, or gives an incorrect answer, the teacher throws the ball to another student.

Crocodile infested river

Divide the class into two groups.

Draw two sets of lines one-and-a-half metres apart – this denotes 'the river'.

Each group must work out how to cross the river without touching it.

If someone touches the ground between the lines, the whole class must start again.

You can vary this activity by widening the river and providing the class with a milk crate and a plank that is not long enough to reach across the river.

Circular ball

You will need a soft ball or bean bag.

The students form a circle, standing at arm's length apart, with a 'leader' in the centre. The leader must try to kick the ball (or bean bag) through one of the gaps between the students.

If the ball gets through, the player on the right of the gap becomes the new leader.

Captain's orders

Certain commands must be explained to the players.

- *Starboard:* everyone moves to the right-hand wall.

- *Port:* everyone moves to the left-hand wall.

- *Scrub the deck:* all crouch and scrub the floor.

- *Numbers (1, 2, 3, 4 and so on):* everyone forms into groups of that number.

On a signal, players follow the commands called out by the teacher or a student nominated to be 'captain'. The commands may be given in any order and at any speed.

Those who make a mistake drop out of the game.